THREE CENTURIES OF PIANO MUSIC

Intermediate Level

18th Century • 19th Century • 20th Century

77 Pieces in Progressive Order

Compiled and Edited by Richard Walters

On the cover:
Detail from *La Camargo Dancing* (c. 1730)
by Nicolas Lancret (1690–1743)

Detail from *Clouds* (1822)
by John Constable (1776–1837)

Detail from *Paris* (1912)
by Konstantin Korovin (1861–1939)

ISBN 978-1-4950-5670-3

G. SCHIRMER, Inc.

DISTRIBUTED BY

HAL•LEONARD®
CORPORATION
7777 W. BLUEMOUND RD. P.O. BOX 13819 MILWAUKEE, WI 53213

www.musicsalesclassical.com
www.halleonard.com

CONTENTS

Though the table of contents appears in alphabetical order by composer,
the music in this book is in progressive order of difficulty within each century.

THE 18TH CENTURY

Anonymous (Baroque)

6   Polonaise in G minor, BWV Appendix 119

2   Minuet in A minor, BWV Appendix 120

Carl Philipp Emanuel Bach

4   March in G Major, BWV Appendix 124

57   Solfeggietto in C minor, H. 220

Johann Sebastian Bach

30   Bourrée from Lute Suite No. 1
      in E minor, BWV 996

60   Prelude in D minor, BWV 926

62   Prelude in F Major, BWV 927

47   Prelude in C minor, BWV 999

Ludwig van Beethoven

12   German Dance in C Major, WoO 8, No. 7

16   German Dance in G Major, WoO 8, No. 6

14   German Dance in B-flat Major,
      WoO 13, No. 2

François Couperin

54   The Little Trifle from *Pièces de clavecin*

Jean-François Dandrieu

37   Lament
      from *Premier livre de pièces de clavecin*

George Frideric Handel

50   Allegro from Suite in G minor, HWV 432

26   Prelude in G Major from *Suite de pièce*,
      Volume 2, No. 9, HWV 442

Franz Joseph Haydn

40   Allegro from Sonata in C Major,
      Hob. XVI/1

Johann Philipp Kirnberger

18   The Chimes

Wolfgang Amadeus Mozart

10   Piece for Clavier in F Major, KV 33B

8   Andantino in E-flat Major, KV 236 (588b)

32   Rondo in C Major, KV 334 (320b)

28   Adagio for Glass Harmonica,
      KV 356 (617a)

9   Funeral March for Signor Maestro
      Contrapunto, KV 453a

24   German Dance in C Major, KV 605, No. 3

Pietro Domenico Paradies (Paradisi)

64   Toccata from Sonata No. 6 in A Major

Jean-Philippe Rameau

34   Tambourin from *Pièces de clavecin*

Domenico Scarlatti

44   Sonata in G Major, L. 79 (K. 391, P. 364)

7   Sonata in D minor, L. 423 (K. 32, P. 14)

Georg Philipp Telemann

20   Cantabile in F Major

THE 19TH CENTURY

Amy Marcy Beach

70   Gavotte in D minor
      from *Children's Album*, Op. 36

Johann Friedrich Burgmüller

82   Gentle Complaint
      from *25 Progressive Studies*, Op. 100

90   Restlessness
      from *25 Progressive Studies*, Op. 100

108   Confidence
      from *18 Characteristic Studies*, Op. 109

Frédéric Chopin

120   Prelude in E minor, Op. 28, No. 4

114   Prelude in B minor, Op. 28, No. 6

111   Prelude in A Major, Op. 28, No. 7

Edvard Grieg

122   Arietta from *Lyric Pieces*, Op. 12

106   Waltz in A minor
      from *Lyric Pieces*, Op. 12

112   Dance of the Elves
      from *Lyric Pieces*, Op. 12

116   Puck from *Lyric Pieces*, Op. 71

Cornelius Gurlitt

92   Hunting Song
      from *Albumleaves for the Young*, Op. 101

87   The Little Wanderer
      from *Albumleaves for the Young*, Op. 101

Stephen Heller

100   Study in A minor (The Avalanche)
      from *25 Melodious Etudes*, Op. 45

Theodor Kullak

78   On the Playground
     from *Scenes from Childhood*, Op. 62

76   Grandmother Tells a Ghost Story
     from *Scenes from Childhood*, Op. 81

Edward MacDowell

74   To a Wild Rose
     from *Woodland Sketches*, Op. 51

Carl Nielsen

98   Folk Melody from *Five Piano Pieces*, Op. 3

Max Reger

96   The Dead Little Bird
     from *Album for Young People*, Op. 17

Robert Schumann

102   Of Strange Lands and People
     from *Scenes from Childhood*, Op. 15

95   Hunting Song
     from *Album for the Young*, Op. 68

110   Little Romance
     from *Album for the Young*, Op. 68

72   The Reaper's Song
     from *Album for the Young*, Op. 68

Pytor Il'yich Tchaikovsky

84   Mazurka in D minor
     from *Album for the Young*, Op. 39

103   Sweet Dream
     from *Album for the Young*, Op. 39

80   The Wooden Soldier's March
     from *Album for the Young*, Op. 39

THE 20TH CENTURY

George Antheil

138   Little Shimmy

Samuel Barber

146   Petite Berceuse

162   To My Steinway
     from *Three Sketches for Pianoforte*

Béla Bartók

140   Bagatelle No. 6
     from *Fourteen Bagatelles*, Sz. 38, BB 50

158   Jeering Song
     from *For Children*, Sz. 42, BB 53

128   Round Dance
     from *For Children*, Sz. 42, BB 53

Paul Creston

129   Festive Dance
     from *Five Little Dances*, Op. 24

136   Rustic Dance
     from *Five Little Dances*, Op. 24

Alan Hovhaness

150   Mountain Lullaby
     from *Mountain Idylls*, Op. 119

Dmitri Kabalevsky

132   The Chase
     from *30 Pieces for Children*, Op. 27

134   Clowning
     from *30 Pieces for Children*, Op. 27

144   Lyric Piece
     from *30 Pieces for Children*, Op. 27

148   Novelette
     from *30 Pieces for Children*, Op. 27

126   Slow Waltz
     from *24 Pieces for Children*, Op. 39

163   Rondo-Toccata
     from *Four Rondos*, Op. 60

Aram Khachaturian

124   Ivan Sings from *Adventures of Ivan*

Robert Muczynski

166   Fable No. 9 from *Fables*, Op. 21

Octavio Pinto

168   Playing Marbles from *Children's Festival:
     Little Suite for the Piano*

Sergei Prokofiev

156   Morning from *Music for Children*, Op. 65

152   Promenade from *Music for Children*, Op. 65

154   Regrets from *Music for Children*, Op. 65

Maurice Ravel

160   Prélude

Dmitri Shostakovich

141   Birthday
     from *Children's Notebook for Piano*, Op. 69

COMPOSER BIOGRAPHIES
AND
NOTES ON THE PIECES

ANONYMOUS
(Baroque Era)

Johann Sebastian Bach included the following pieces (BWV Appendix 119 and 120) in the second volume, dated 1725, of *The Notebook for Anna Magdalena Bach*. The notebooks (the first was begun in 1722) were for Bach's second wife, Anna Magdalena, who was much younger than the composer. Such keyboard notebooks of assembled favorite pieces were common in Baroque homes, and used for family music-making. (They are the equivalent of the modern published music collection, such as this one.) Some of the pieces in the Anna Magdalena notebook are by J.S. Bach; others are not. Previously attributed to Bach, we now know that the pieces below are not J.S. Bach compositions. The composers are unknown. We can assume that they date from the first decades of the eighteenth century and are likely German in origin.

Polonaise in G minor, BWV Appendix 119
A polonaise stems from Polish folk dances. The term began to be used in the seventeenth century primarily by composers outside Poland. Originally a vocal form, by the time of Bach it had become an instrumental form characterized by triple meter and short repeated sections. The polonaise was later developed in the Romantic period, notably by Chopin. Articulation has been editorially suggested in this edition to help achieve a Baroque style. Ornamentation is possible in this style. We have noted two places where a trill is optional.

Minuet in A minor, BWV Appendix 120
This has a contemplative quality, unusual for a minuet. This piece is in two large, obvious sections, both repeated. A few slurs of brief notes to be played *legato* have been indicated as editorial suggestions. The general touch for this piece might be described as *portato*, which is a slightly detached touch. Trills begin on the note above in every case. The composer has given no tempo. Pedal probably should be avoided.

GEORGE ANTHEIL
(1900–1959, American)

After studying with Constantin von Sternberg in Philadelphia and Ernest Bloch in New York, American composer George Antheil moved to Berlin in 1922. He travelled around Europe as a concert pianist, often performing his own works. In 1923 he moved to Paris, where he became a prominent member of the avant-garde, befriending James Joyce, Ezra Pound, W.B. Yeats, Erik Satie and Pablo Picasso. His most famous piece is *Ballet mécanique* (1925), scored for multiple pianos, player pianos, percussion, siren, and two propellers. Due to the practical performance issues, it is known more theoretically than for actual performance. Antheil's earlier works were often jazz-inspired, experimental and jarringly mechanistic. In the 1940s, back in the United States, Antheil turned to a more conventional style. A virtuoso concert pianist, he composed more for piano than any other instrument.

Little Shimmy (composed 1923)
"Little Shimmy" was composed in the same year as Antheil's professional debut as a concert pianist (at the Théâtre des Champs-Elysées in Paris), and Antheil may have played it on this recital, a great success attended by his illustrious supporters, such as James Joyce, Erik Satie, Ezra Pound, Jean Cocteau and Darius Milhaud. Classical composers in the U.S., as well as in Paris and Berlin, were discovering American jazz and blues in this period and incorporating those sounds into compositions. "Little Shimmy" is an example of just such a piece by a young American composer living in Paris. Antheil indicated neither tempo nor dynamics. Editorial suggestions are in brackets. The dotted eighth-note/sixteenth-note combination is like a "swing beat. Note that the deliberately insistent and shrill high treble diads in measures 12 and 14 are straight eighth notes, not swing beat.

CARL PHILIPP EMANUEL BACH
(1714–1788, German)

Carl Philipp Emanuel Bach, second son of Johann Sebastian Bach, was a major composer bridging the distinctions between late Baroque and early Classical periods, writing in the *empfindsamer Stil* (sensitive style), meaning an emotionally turbulent or dynamically expressive compositional style, as distinguished from the more restrained Rococo musical style. Carl received music lessons from his father until he began studies in law at Leipzig University and continued in Frankfurt. After graduation, C.P.E. Bach accepted a position in the court orchestra of Crown Prince Frederick of Prussia and moved to Berlin. In 1768 C.P.E. Bach became the music director of sacred music for the city of Hamburg, a position previously held by his godfather, Georg Philipp Telemann. C.P.E. Bach was extraordinarily prolific, writing over 1,000 works for voices and keyboard instruments.

March in G Major, BWV Appendix 124
(composed 1725 or earlier)
This march, included in the second volume of *The Notebook for Anna Magdalena Bach*, is usually attributed to C.P.E. Bach. We have made editorial suggestions regarding articulation and dynamics which will bring the style of the piece to life. The trills in measures 7 and 20 should begin on the note above. Do not use pedal in playing this march.

Solfeggietto in C minor, H. 220 (composed 1766)
C.P.E. Bach generally wrote in the more "modern" *stile galante*, not the contrapuntal high Baroque style of his famous father Johann Sebastian Bach. However, in this Solfeggieto from 1766, he harkens back to the earlier Baroque style. Most of the piece has a single note sounding at a time, with running sixteenth notes that outline harmonic movement. The implied harmony generally changes every two beats, on beats 1 and 3. For dramatic effect, at the climax of the piece (measures 21–24) the composer stops changing the harmony every two beats and instead sustains the harmony through the entire measure. The technical challenge is to pass the sixteenth notes from hand to hand and maintain absolute evenness in touch and rhythm. Though a valid approach would be to use no pedal throughout the entire piece, some pianists may wish to experiment with light pedal, with the half notes and whole notes in the bass line as a signal for pedaling.

JOHANN SEBASTIAN BACH
(1685–1750, German)

One of the greatest composers in the history of music, J. S. Bach defined the high Baroque style, developing counterpoint in composition further than any composer before him or since. However, during his lifetime he was more known for his virtuoso organ and harpsichord playing than for composition. Relatively few people were familiar with the works of J.S. Bach in the decades after his death. The modern wide recognition of Bach as a master composer began in the mid-nineteenth century, decades after his death, first championed by Felix Mendelssohn. Throughout his life Bach wrote keyboard music for his students, including his children. Bach composed hundreds of works, most for practical occasions, including cantatas, oratorios, motets, various instrumental suites, harpsichord works, organ works, and orchestral pieces. He came from a long line of musicians, and was father to six noted composers.

Prelude in D minor, BWV 926
(composition date unknown)
Bach gave us no tempo marking for this piece. However, there is a clue as to what your individual tempo should be. Look at the fast moving sixteenth notes in measures 39–42. The performance tempo at which you ultimately arrive is determined by how well you can master these measures. This edition includes Bach's original few markings regarding articulation, notably the *legato* slurs in measures 9–10 and 13–14. Other than this, Bach gave us no articulation. Performance practice during the period would have taken care of other articulation expected in the piece. The quarter notes which appear in the left hand in measures 10, 14, and 20–38 should be played with slight separation. Likewise, the moving eighth notes in the right hand, except when marked by Bach with slurs as *legato*, should also be played with a slight separation. The mordent which appears on the downbeat of measure 1 in the left hand may be played either beginning on the beat, or beginning slightly before the beat. In a slower tempo, a mordent such as this would always begin on the beat.

Prelude in F Major, BWV 927
(composed between 1737 and 1741)
Notice that there are no *legato* slurs anywhere in this piece. All eighth notes, including the diads in measures 1–4, should be played with slight separation. This also applies to the single eighth notes in the left hand in measures 5–8 and other places. Perpetual motion of sixteenth notes is common in Bach, requiring absolute steadiness and evenness. The ending in measures 14 and 15 is reminiscent of a toccata, a sudden bit of freedom breaking up the mood and musical texture of the piece.

Bourrée from Lute Suite No. 1 in E minor, BWV 996
(composition date unknown)
A *bourrée* is a lively dance movement, French in origin from the Baroque, always in 2/2 or 4/4 meter, and in binary form. A *bourrée* always begins with a quarter note upbeat. A *bourrée* became an optional part of the standard Baroque suite. Though the *bourrée* fell out of favor after the Baroque period among composers, the original folk dance is still found in the Auvergne region of France. There is no tempo indication in Bach's manuscript. In keeping with a traditional *bourée*, we have suggested *Allegro moderato*. Bach indicated no dynamics or articulations in his manuscript. There are editorial suggestions about these details which will help create appropriate Baroque style. We recommend no sustaining pedal.

Prelude in C minor, BWV 999 (composed c. 1720)
This piece uses the same rhythmic structure throughout except in the last two measures. The harmonic movement is the propelling factor in this piece, with the harmony changing for each measure. If you would like to see the harmonic progression Bach has created, you can play all of the notes in any measure together as a chord. Do not use pedal in this piece. There should be calmness in performance even though the music is quite busy.

SAMUEL BARBER
(1910–1981, American)

Born in Pennsylvania, Samuel Barber was a precocious musical talent who composed from an early age, and at fourteen began studies in singing, piano, and composition at the Curtis Institute. One of the most prominent American composers of the twentieth century, he is remembered for his distinctive neo-Romantic style. Early in his career he performed as a singer, which may have helped him develop an aptitude for writing the lyrical melodies that define his works. Barber wrote for orchestra, voice, choir, piano, chamber ensemble, and solo instruments and was well acclaimed during his lifetime. After 1938, almost all of his compositions were written on commission from renowned performers and ensembles. Among his well-known pieces are the *Adagio for Strings* (1936), the opera *Vanessa* (1956–57), *Knoxville: Summer of 1915* (1947), and *Hermit Songs* (1953).

Petite Berceuse (composed c. 1923)

This piece by the thirteen year old Samuel Barber showed marked progress in his compositions. It remained unpublished in his lifetime. It was first published in *Samuel Barber: Early Piano Works* (2010), and also included in *Samuel Barber: Complete Piano Music, Revised Edition.* Barber's music in general, including this piece, is about a strong sense of melodic phrase. There is some *rubato* (slight relaxing or surging of tempo) implied in this romantic piece, although the composer has written most of this in (measures 8–9, 15–17, 26–32). However, keep it simple (*dolce semplice*). Note the editorial suggestions for pedaling.

To My Steinway from *Three Sketches for Pianoforte* (composed 1923–24)

Barber's father published *Three Sketches for Pianoforte* in a private, very limited edition in 1924, but in practical terms they remained unpublished and unavailable in the composer's lifetime. The set was posthumously published in *Samuel Barber: Early Piano Works* (2010), and also included in *Samuel Barber: Complete Piano Music, Revised Edition.* "To My Steinway" is the second piece in the set, composed in June of 1923, when Barber was thirteen years old. It is dedicated "to Number 230601," the manufacturing number on the Steinway piano his parents had given him. Barber's love for the piano, and for piano literature the piece echoes, is obvious. Context determines how fast or slow a chord should be rolled. In this Adagio piece, the chords should not be rolled too quickly. Think of them as beautiful harmony to be savored, emerging from the lowest note to the top note.

BÉLA BARTÓK

(1881–1945, Hungarian; became a US citizen in 1945)

Béla Bartók is one of the most important and often performed composers of the twentieth century, and much of his music, including *Concerto for Orchestra*, his concertos, his string quartets, his opera *Bluebeard's Castle*, and his piano music are firmly in the classical repertoire. His parents were amateur musicians who nurtured their young son with exposure to dance music, drumming, and piano lessons. In 1899 he started piano and composition studies at the Academy of Music in Budapest and not long after graduation he joined the Academy's piano faculty. Bartók wished to create music that was truly Hungarian at its core, a desire that sparked his deep interest in folk music. His work collecting and studying folksongs from around the Baltic region impacted his own compositional style greatly in terms of rhythm, mood, and texture.

Bartók utilized folk influences to create a distinctive style. Though he composed opera, concertos, ballets, and chamber music, he was also committed to music education and composed several piano works for students, including his method *Mikrokosmos*. Bartók toured extensively in the 1920s and '30s, and became well-known as both a pianist and composer. He immigrated to the US in 1940 to escape war and political turmoil in Europe, and settled in New York City, though the last years of his life were difficult, with many health problems.

Bagatelle No. 6 from *Fourteen Bagatelles*, Sz. 38, BB 50 (composed 1908)

Bartók stated the following about the Fourteen Bagatelles of 1908. "In these, a new piano style appears as a reaction to the exuberance of the romantic piano music of the nineteenth century, a style stripped of all unessential decorative elements, using only the most restricted technical means. As later developments show, the Bagatelles inaugurate a new trend of piano writing in my career, which is consistently followed in almost all of my successive piano works." This pensive Bagatelle is an excellent introduction to Bartók's lyrical modernism, an individual style which was forming in the early twentieth century. A pianist should pay careful attention to all Bartók's details of dynamics, decrescendos, accents, diminuendo.

Selections from *For Children*, Sz. 42, BB 53 (composed 1908–09)

Bartók was one of the pioneering ethnomusicologists in Eastern Europe, collecting and documenting thousands of folksongs from Hungary and neighboring countries. The original edition of *For Children* was in four volumes. Volumes 1–2 were compositions based on Hungarian folksongs. Volumes 3–4 were compositions based on Slovakian folksongs. Bartók created a revised edition in 1943, with only minor changes to the original regarding compositional content, with the pieces retitled. Some pieces were eliminated for the revised edition, and the four volumes were consolidated into two. In the preface to *For Children* Bartók wrote that the pieces were designed to teach young players "the simple and non-Romantic beauties of folk music."

Jeering Song (Volume 1)

From Volume 2 in the original four volume edition, with the English title "Wedding Day." Bartók changed the title for the revised edition. When the melody of Section 1 returns for Section 3, notice how Bartók placed different accents, stressing beat 2 rather than beat 1 the second time. This adds playfulness to the "jeering." Bartók has added possible grace notes in the *ossia* (optional). Bartók surely knew that these grace notes would be problematic for some student pianists. Carefully observe the dynamics the composer has written, which feature sharp contrasts.

Round Dance (Volume 1)

From Volume 1 in the original four volume edition, with the English title "The Girl in White." Bartók changed the title for the revised edition. Notice that Bartók intends that the pedal is cleared after the second left-hand chord is played in measures 1–7. This very specific pedaling helps create the phrasing in each measure. Though it is *Lento*, Bartók's indication of quarter note = 70 doesn't feel extremely slow.

AMY MARCY BEACH
(1867–1944, American)

Amy Beach (her maiden name was Amy Cheney) was one of the first female composers to be recognized with success in the United States. She composed her first piano piece at age four. Her first published piece came at age sixteen. That same year she made a debut as a pianist with the Boston Symphony. Her many works include the *Gaelic Symphony*, a piano concerto, the opera *Cabildo*, many piano pieces, chamber music, and over 150 art songs. Beach was deeply interested in theory and composition, and translated various treatises from French and German. In 1892 she became the first female composer to have a piece performed by the New York Symphony. After the death of her husband in 1910, she composed and performed for the rest of her life, and was a leading cultural figure of her day. Beach had the condition of synesthesia, a neurological association of color with sound.

Gavotte in D minor, from *Children's Album*, Op. 36 (No.2) (composed 1897)
This is one of five pieces in *Children's Album*. A gavotte was a dance movement in the Baroque Era, generally in 2/2 time, characterized by regular phrasing, binary form, and in a moderate tempo. As a Baroque dance movement, a gavotte was slower than a bourrée, rigaudon, or gigue. Composers after the Baroque period used the label "gavotte" vaguely, and virtually none of the Baroque characteristics were retained. Beach probably meant a light dancelike quality for this piece in giving it this title. The spots marked *sopra* in measures 23 and 38 mean that the right hand crosses the left hand, but just barely.

LUDWIG VAN BEETHOVEN
(1770–1827, German)

Beethoven was the major figure of the transition from the Classical era to the Romantic era in European music. As one of the first successful freelance composers, as opposed to a composer thriving in a royal court appointment, Beethoven wrote widely in nearly every genre of his day, with emphasis on instrumental music. He acquired wealth and fame beyond any composer before him. Beethoven's chamber music, piano sonatas, concertos and symphonies are part of the ever present international repertoire. In his youth he was regarded as one of the greatest pianists of his time, but he stopped performing after hearing loss set in. He devoted an enormous amount of his compositional efforts to the piano, which as an instrument came of age during his lifetime. He was occasionally a piano teacher, with wealthy patrons and young prodigies begging for lessons, though this task was not a match for his nature. However, teaching piano did inspire him to write many pieces for students.

German Dance in G Major, WoO 8, No. 6
(composed 1795)
The rustic quality to this dance gives it the feeling of a *ländler*. The composer has given us no tempo; this is open for interpretation. We recommend *allegro moderato*. The tempo at which measures 13–15 can be played smoothly and without struggle is as fast as the entire piece should be played. By nature a dance is a rhythmic piece of music. Notice the variety of articulation, dynamics, and accents. We recommend no pedal to allow for clarity of execution.

German Dance in C Major, WoO 8, No. 7
(composed 1795)
This is music with character and high spirits. It moves from elegance, such as in the long phrases in the opening, to boisterous rambunctiousness in the section around measure 25. Style comes from articulation, as is true in all Classical era pieces. Note the sharp and sudden changes in dynamics. Tempo is open to interpretation since Beethoven provided no indication. An acceptable tempo might range from quarter note = 130 to 168.

German Dance in B-flat Major, WoO 13, No. 2
(composition date unknown, probably before 1800)
This dance is akin to the third movement minuet and trio, or scherzo and trio, of a Classical symphony. The music is in three large sections, the second section being the trio that begins in measure 17. The *marcato* markings in the right hand in the first few measures are a period indication of *staccato* that is pronounced and with accent. Beethoven gave no tempo indication, which leaves this open for interpretation. We have recommended *allegro moderato* because of the character of the music.

JOHANN FRIEDRICH BURGMÜLLER
(1806–1874, German/French)

The Burgmüllers were a musical family. Johann August Franz, the patriarch, was a composer and musical theatre director as well as the founder of the Lower Rhine Music Festival. Johann Friedrich's brother Norbert was a child prodigy at the piano and a composer. Johann Freidrich distinguished himself from his family by leaving Germany and establishing a career in Parisian circles as a composer of French salon music. Later in life he withdrew from performing and focused on teaching. He wrote many short character pieces for his students as etudes. Several collections of these are perennial favorites of piano teachers, especially opus 100, 105, and 109.

Gentle Complaint (Douce Plainte)
from *25 Progressive Studies*
(*25 Études faciles et progressive*), Op. 100 (No. 16)
This mood is a combination of weary discontent and agitation. Burgmüller creates interest in the first few measures by having a long melody in one hand, and a short,

agitated, nervous figure in the other hand. The melody passes to the left hand at the end of measure 5 and back to the right hand on beat 2 of measure 7. The sixteenth notes in the left hand in measure 1, and other places like it, are a bubbling murmur, supporting the melody. Burgmüller asks for dramatic changes of dynamics in the second page of the music, accumulating in *f* in measure 14, and then quickly back down to *p* two measures later. This piece disappears without calling attention to its ending.

Restlessness (Inquiétude) from *25 Progressive Studies, (25 Études faciles et progressive)*, Op. 100 (No.18)
Burgmüller has created a mood of agitation. The simple elements are staccato chords in the left hand answered by three slurred sixteenth notes in the right hand. Notice the *subito f* in the second ending in measure 25; the texture of the left hand changes here as the composer asks the pianist to slur rather than play staccato.

Confidence from *18 Characteristic Studies (18 Études de genre)*, Op. 109 (No. 1)
True confidence is moving forward with quiet self-assurance, and sureness of motion certainly is characterized in this music. Even though there is busyness created by the triplet figure, the top voice in the right hand and left hand give us quarter notes that move smoothly forward. The Romantic qualities of the piece are not only in its harmony, but in the swells of emotion which are indicated in the *crescendos*, *decrescendos*, and dramatic changes to dynamics.

FRÉDÉRIC CHOPIN
(1810–1849, Polish/French)

A major Romantic era composer for piano, Chopin created a uniquely personal, forward-thinking style, and revolutionized literature for the instrument. He left his native Poland at age 20 after an education at the Warsaw Conservatory, first briefly to Vienna before settling in Paris for most of the remainder of his life. Chopin became a much sought after piano teacher in the French capital, and was part of the lively salon culture, where he preferred to perform instead of in large concert halls. He is reputed to have had an extremely refined, poetic touch as a pianist. He was in chronic frail health through much of his adult life, and died at the young age of 39, probably brought on by tuberculosis. Because of political upheaval, Chopin was never able to return to Poland, and his nostalgic ache for his homeland is a characteristic heard in his music.

The Preludes (composed 1836–39)
In music a prelude could be one of two descriptions. It might simply be introductory material to something that follows it. Chopin's preludes are not an introduction, but stand alone on their own. However, they follow the tradition of the genre which establishes the key of a piece. This tradition comes from Bach's famous preludes and fugues. Like Bach, Chopin wrote 24 preludes, one in each of the major and minor keys. The 24 preludes were composed between the years 1836–39. In autumn

of 1838 Chopin was staying on the island of Majorca with the writer George Sand. After the onset of illness he was taken to a deserted monastery near the town of Palma, where most of the composition was completed for the 24 Preludes.

Prelude in E minor, Op. 28, No. 4
Most would agree that this Prelude is characterized by quiet but disturbed contemplation, briefly rising to a surge of hot emotion, then falling back into pondering resignation. The composer's indication of *espressivo* at the top of the piece invites a performer to arrive at an individual interpretation, and there are many ways to interpret this prelude. Chopin intends that the first 11 measures are to be played softly. There is a *crescendo* into the deceptive cadence in measure 21. (A deceptive cadence is one in which the harmony resolves in a surprising way.) Chopin's marking of *stretto*, beginning in measure 16, indicates that he intends for the tempo to press forward in this short section, relaxing back to the *tempo primo* heading into measure 19.

Prelude in B minor, Op. 28, No. 6
The left hand plays a single note melody throughout and the right hand is the accompaniment. The only section in which the right hand might be considered to have taken the melody is the top voice beginning on the third beat of measure 6 through the second beat of measure 8. Except for this, the texture is the same throughout, with the lower voice in the right hand in quarter notes and the upper voice is repeated eighth notes. Sometimes it helps a pianist to find inspiration in imagining another instrument playing the music. Imagine the richness of a cello playing the left-hand melody, and also the legato that instrument would naturally bring to it.

Prelude in A Major, Op. 28, No. 7
This prelude is as if a graceful waltz has been put under a microscope, slowed down and contemplated at leisure. It is almost like a wistful, nostalgic memory. The volume increases only at the point of the surprising change of harmony on the downbeat of measure 12. Note that the pedal clears for the quarter-note pickup that begins the next phrase. This Prelude is a brief piece of loveliness. It would be a great mistake to play it too quickly.

FRANÇOIS COUPERIN
(1668–1733, French)

François was the son of the organist at Saint Gervais church in Paris. His father died when the boy was ten. Saint Gervais not only saved his father's position for the budding young musician and paid for his musical education, the church also paid for the housing and upkeep of François and his mother until he was old enough to assume the duties as full-time organist in 1688. In this period the royal court controlled all copyrights. Couperin obtained permission to publish his music. He was appointed organist of the King in 1693 and began teaching harpsichord to much of Parisian aristocracy. For the rest of his life he was regarded as one of the greatest teachers and keyboard players in France. Couperin published four books of harpsichord pieces, considered as landmarks of the French Baroque style. He was the author of a definitive treatise, *The Art of Harpsichord Playing*, addressing fingering, touch, ornamentation and various other aspects of keyboard technique.

The Little Trifle (Le Petit-Rien) (published the third *Pièces de clavecin collection*, 1722) from *Pièces de clavecin*, the fourteenth order of Harpsichord Pieces
This piece has the structure of a simple rondo. A rondo (rondeau) is music with a recurring theme, with other musical material in between theme statements. The theme is measures 1–16. This recurs in measures 25–40 and 59–74. The composer has given us a marking of *légérement*, which means lightly, but does not address tempo. The Baroque style in France was different from the familiar German style of Bach and the Italian style of Scarlatti. French Baroque music is often much more heavily ornamented. If the ornamentation is challenging, a suggestion is to play only the right hand ornaments and omit the left hand ornaments. Articulation needs to be carefully considered. We have suggested staccatos on eighth notes such as in measure 1, which is part of the style and will help achieve the lightness that Couperin has requested. Any pedal will smear the music and undermine necessary clarity.

PAUL CRESTON
(1906–1985, American)

Paul Creston was born into a poor Italian immigrant family in New York. As a child he took piano and organ lessons but was self-taught in theory and composition. In 1938 Creston was awarded a Guggenheim Fellowship, and in 1941 the New York Music Critics' Circle Award. He served as the director of A.S.C.A.P. from 1960–1968, and was composer-in-residence and professor of music at Central Washington State College from 1968–1975. His works, which include orchestral, vocal, piano, and chamber music repertoire, often feature shifting rhythmic patterns. He wrote a number of solos for instruments customarily left out of the limelight, such as the marimba, accordion, or saxophone. Creston was an important composition teacher (John Corigliano studied with him), and also wrote the books *Principles of Rhythm* and *Rational Metric Notation*.

Rustic Dance, from *Five Little Dances*, Op. 24 (No. 1)
(composed 1940)
Notice how the texture changes from accented, loud and *non legato* to smooth and soft in measure 13. The composer's marking "Heavily" and the title "Rustic Dance" should help in finding the character of the music.

Festive Dance, No. 5 from *Five Little Dances*, Op. 24 (No. 5) (composed 1940)
Pay careful attention to the composer's marking of both *strongly rhythmic* and *legato*. Sharp dynamic contrasts (from *f* to a sudden *p*, for instance) are part of the

character of the music. The composer has indicated dotted quarter note = 96. It's possible to take the piece at a quicker pace, but be careful not to take it too quickly. Use no sustaining pedal throughout.

JEAN-FRANÇOIS DANDRIEU
(1681 or 82–1738, French)

Dandrieu became organist at Saint-Merri in Paris in 1704. He had established himself prior to this as a competent keyboard player. The composer was also the organist for St. Barthélemy and the royal chapel. He is remembered today for his books of harpsichord pieces, which capture the French Baroque style most similar to that of Couperin.

Lament (La Gémissante)
(*Premier livre de pièces de clavecin*, published 1724)
from the *Premier livre de pieces de clavecin* (*Harpsichord Pieces Book 1*), second suite of Harpsichord Pieces
The composer has indicated that the piece should be played tenderly. The musical structure is essentially a rondo. The theme is measures 1–16. This recurs in measures 26–41 and 50–65. We might recommend that the repeat of the first section be omitted. Essentially this is a song-like melody in the right hand. We have suggested historically stylistic articulation that makes the slurring different in the right hand melody from the accompaniment figure in the left hand. Unlike most Baroque music, this particular piece may benefit from discreet use of the sustaining pedal, but it must be used with subtlety and remain inconspicuous.

EDVARD GRIEG
(1843–1907, Norwegian)

Grieg was the great Norwegian composer of the nineteenth century. After childhood in Bergen in a richly musical family he entered the Leipzig Conservatory at age 15, where he was exposed to the major German musicians and composers of the day. He returned to Norway at age 19, and soon became acquainted with Norwegian folk music, which would be the source of inspiration for his individual musical style. Recognition as a composer and pianist led to Grieg's appointment as conductor of the Philharmonic Society in Oslo; he also founded the Norwegian Academy of Music. Through travel and musical connections he became a part of the international music scene of his day, in contact with many major musical figures. Grieg was an excellent pianist, and his piano music shows an idiomatic understanding of the instrument. The *Lyric Pieces* (*Lyrische Stücke*) are short character works composed in nine sets from 1867 to 1901.

Arietta from *Lyric Pieces*, Op. 12 (No. 1)
(composed 1867)
An arietta is a short aria for a singer, and this piece is reminiscent of a song. The top note of the right hand is the melody and everything else is a supporting

accompaniment. There are three voices: the afore-mentioned melody on top, the bass note, and the middle voice, which passes from left hand to right. Like many Romantic period pieces, this one asks for gentle, flowing graceful playing. Though Grieg asks the pianist to do some swells of volume here and there, the entire piece is marked *p*. Note Grieg's specific pedaling indications.

Waltz in A minor from *Lyric Pieces*, Op. 12 (No. 2) (composed 1866)

Not all of Grieg's music has Norwegian nationalistic folk influence, but it is strongly present in this waltz, which has a playful, dance-like quality. The melody leads throughout. Grieg has given very specific pedaling for the accompanying figure in the left hand, slurring beats on the "and" of 2 and clearing the pedal for beat 3, which is separated.

Dance of the Elves from *Lyric Pieces*, Op. 12 (No. 4) (composed 1867)

One cannot help but be reminded of the most famous fairy music of the nineteenth century, Mendelssohn's *A Midsummer Night's Dream*, which has the same light, minor key, dance-like character as Grieg's "Dance of the Elves." All eighth notes are to be played slurred and all quarter notes staccato. The only exceptions are quarter notes that occur within a phrase in the left hand in measures 7–8, 15–16, 37–38, and 59–60. Pedal should only be used in the three places the composer marked.

Puck from *Lyric Pieces*, Op. 71 (No. 3) (composed 1901)

Puck, from Shakespeare's play *A Midsummer Night's Dream*, is head henchman to Oberon, king of the fairies. (Puck is also known as Robin Goodfellow.) He is a mischievous character with supernatural powers. At one point in the play he states that he will "put a girdle around the earth in forty minutes." The full measure rests, such as measures 17 and 76, are playful indications of Puck's character. Grieg has written many details of articulation and dynamics, all of which must be carefully observed. His tempo indication of a half note = 176 is extremely fast, faster than many can play this piece.

CORNELIUS GURLITT
(1820–1901, German)

Many of Gurlitt's piano works have colorful, descriptive names, which is not surprising for someone with a lifelong interest in art. He studied music in Leipzig, Copenhagen and Rome, where he was nominated an honorary member of the papal academy Di Santa Cecilia. His brother Louis was a very successful artist in Rome, and Cornelius also studied painting for a time while living there. Gurlitt worked as a pianist and church organist, and also served as a military band master. He returned to his home town of Altona, where the Duke of Augustenburg hired him as music teacher for three of his daughters. Gurlitt wrote symphonies, songs, operas and cantatas, but is bester remembered for his piano pieces for students.

The Little Wanderer (Der kleine Wandersmann) from *Albumleaves for the Young (Albumblätter für die Jugend)*, Op. 101 (No. 12)

Even though it is more complex than a simple three-part form, it feels in three large sections: measures 1–25, measures 26–40, and measures 41 to the end. Imagine a happy traveler humming while walking. The traveler perhaps encounters some stormy weather in the middle section, but it subsides with the return of the music of the opening section.

Hunting Song (Jagdstück) from *Albumleaves for the Young (Albumblätter für die Jugend)*, Op. 101 (No. 19)

Portrayals of hunting with bugle calls are not uncommon in pieces from the 19th century particularly. Hunting calls are normally broken arpeggios of some kind, such as the opening E-flat harmony (the traditional hunting key). The piece is a pleasure to play without many technical obstacles. Ponder what Gurlitt means by the *crescendo* and *accelerando* in measures 35–39, followed by the long rest with a fermata. Is this a climax of the hunt?

GEORGE FRIDERIC HANDEL
(1685–1759, German/British)

Handel was one of the defining composers of the Baroque period. After a brief time in Italy as a young man, he spent nearly his entire adult career in London, where he became famous as a composer of opera and oratorio, including *Messiah*, now his most recognizable music. Handel also wrote numerous concertos, suites, overtures, cantatas, trio sonatas, and solo keyboard works. Though he taught some students early in his career and occasionally instructed members of the London aristocracy, Handel was not known for his teaching abilities. His keyboard works were likely not written for any of his students, but to fulfill commissions or generate income from publication. Handel composed various keyboard works until 1720, when he became master of the orchestra for the Royal Academy of Music, an organization dedicated to performing new operas. After Italian opera fell out of vogue in London, Handel turned his compositional efforts to oratorio.

Allegro from Suite in G minor, HWV 432 (composed before 1720, published in 1720)

As with many faster Baroque keyboard pieces, this movement is about maintaining steadiness throughout. As with many other Baroque pieces like it, it is not much about dynamic contrasts. We have made stylistic suggestion about articulation of eighth notes, which should be played with slight separation. Even though the music is quite busy, a good performance of it ultimately has a sense of calm about it.

Prelude in G Major from *Suite de pièce*, Volume 2, No. 9, HWV 442 (composed c. 1703–06)

Articulation and steadiness are the key factors in this Prelude. We have suggested that some eighth notes be played staccato, and some in two-note slurs, which will create appropriate style. The quarter notes should be played slightly detached. At an *allegro* tempo, the sixteenth notes by default will be played slurred. The touch should be light, refined, and elegant, and the mood joyous.

FRANZ JOSEPH HAYDN
(1732–1809, Austrian)

One of the major composers of the eighteenth century, Haydn defined the sound of the Classical style. He was employed by the Esterházy court for the majority of his career, serving two Princes from the Hungarian ruling family in Vienna as well as in Hungary. Later in his life, Haydn spent time in London composing for the German violinist and musical impresario Johann Peter Salomon (1745–1815). Haydn lived his last years in Vienna. He wrote in nearly every genre of his day including operas, symphonies, and chamber music. Though his keyboard music is not as well-known as his orchestral works, he wrote over 50 piano sonatas and a large assortment of other keyboard pieces. Haydn's influence in Classical era music is captured in the pet name by which he became known in his later life, "Papa Haydn," a term of endearment bestowed upon him by the hundreds of musicians who had learned from him. The nickname also refers to Haydn being the compositional father of the modern symphony.

Allegro from Sonata in C Major, Hob. XVI/1
(attributed to Haydn, composed 1750–55)
This *Allegro* makes frequent use of ornaments, such as the mordent in measure 1 and the turn in measure 22. The mordent in measure 1 (beat 1) recurs many times. At *allegro* it always begun on the beat, not before the beat, starting on the principal note and then quickly moves to the lower note and back up. Ornaments at this tempo are played quickly. You can see the realization written out in small notes above the right hand for the turn in measure 22. The trill in measure 45 should begin on the note above.

STEPHEN HELLER
(1813–1888, Hungarian/French)

Heller begged his parents for piano lessons as a child. At the age of seven he was already writing music for a small band put together by his father. The boy was sent to Vienna to study with Carl Czerny, but quickly found the lessons too expensive and instead studied with Anton Halm, who introduced Heller to Beethoven and Schubert. At the age of 13, Heller was giving concerts in Vienna as a pianist and two years later began touring Europe. His travels brought him in contact with Chopin, Liszt, Paganini, and most importantly Robert Schumann, with whom he developed a life-long friendship. Heller even contributed to Schumann's journal *Neue Zeitschrift* under the pseudonym Jeanquirit. After two years of touring, the rigorous schedule became too much for the boy and Heller settled first in Ausburg, and then in Paris to teach and compose. He wrote several hundred piano pieces, of which the short character pieces from opuses 45, 46, and 47 are frequently performed today.

Study in A minor ("The Avalanche")
from *25 Melodious Etudes (25 Études mélodiques)*, Op. 45 (No. 2) (composed 1844)
The knickname "The Avalanche" does not appear in the first edition, but somehow the piece has become known by that name. It is interesting to note that the "avalanche" does not begin with downward movement, but upward movement. Perhaps Heller had in mind the frenzied running away from the sudden avalanche. The most characteristic musical gesture is the three-note slur in the left hand then in the right hand. This gesture is repeated again and again, whether going up or down. There is a great deal of drama in this brief piece.

ALAN HOVHANESS
(1911–2000, American)

Alan Hovhaness was born in Somerville, Massachusetts, and studied at the New England Conservatory with Frederick Converse. He became interested in the music of India, to which he was exposed by musicians in the Boston area, and later looked to his Armenian heritage as well as music from Japan and Korea for inspiration. A prolific composer, Hovhaness' over five hundred works include all the major genres of western art music. He wrote six ballets as well as other stage works, sixty-six symphonies, works for chorus and voice, and numerous chamber and piano pieces. One of his most well-known works is his Symphony No. 2 *Mysterious Mountain*, premiered by Leopold Stokowski and the Philadelphia Orchestra in 1955. His career went through a number of stages, incorporating aspects from the Renaissance and the Romantic era in addition to traditions outside Western classical music. Despite these shifts in style, he consistently sought to portray a connection between music, spirituality, and nature. Mountains particularly moved him, and he chose to live much of his life in Switzerland and the Pacific Northwest due to the proximity of these regions to the landscape that served as his muse.

Mountain Lullaby from *Mountain Idylls*, Op. 119 (No. 3) (composed 1955)
This set was subtitled "Three Easy Pieces for Piano." Published as set in 1955, the three pieces were written at various times, with "Mountain Lullaby" composed in 1955. An idyll is a poem describing a pastoral, simple scene. Hovhaness was particularly fond of mountains. Chromaticism and dissonance is part of twentieth century style. The composer has written very specific pedaling that must be explicitly observed for the character of this quietly mysterious piece to emerge.

DMITRI KABALEVSKY
(1904–1987, Russian)

Kabalevsky was an important Russian composer of the Soviet era who wrote music in many genres, including four symphonies, a handful of operas, theatre and film scores, patriotic music, choral music, vocal music, and numerous piano works. He embraced the Soviet notion of socialist realism in art, a fact that was more than politically advantageous to his career in the USSR. While studying piano and composition at the Moscow Conservatory, he taught piano lessons at a music college and it was for these students that he began writing works for progressing players. In 1932 he began teaching at the Moscow Conservatory, earning the title of professor in 1939. He eventually went on to develop programs for the concert hall, radio, and television aimed at teaching children about classical music. In the last decades of his life, Kabalevsky focused on developing music curricula for schools, retiring from the Moscow Conservatory to teach in public schools where he could test his theories and the effectiveness of his syllabi. This he considered his true life's work, and his pedagogical principles revolutionized music education in Russia. A collection of his writings on music education was published in English in 1988 as *Music and Education: A Composer Writes About Musical Education.*

Selections from *30 Pieces for Children,* Op. 27
(composed 1937–38)

Kabalevsky often quoted Maxim Gorki, saying that books for children should be "the same as for adults, only better." Kabalevsky believed strongly in writing music for students that was not dumbed-down, but rather, complete, imaginative compositions unto themselves. Kabalevsky did a slight revision of Op. 27 in 1985, which was intended to be an authoritative edition. (This is our source for the pieces in this collection.)

Clowning (No. 10)

Kabalevsky was a master at writing pieces for students that sound brilliant without being overly difficult. Notice the articulation pattern almost throughout: a staccato eighth note in the left hand answered by two slurred eighth notes in the right hand. The composer asks for a tenuto stress and pedaling on the dotted half note at the end of a phrase, ending the phrase with a different tone color. Dynamic contrasts are very clear and should be crisply observed. Notice the soft pedal (*una corda*) in measures 25–32, and again in 43–44, which will also give a different tone color. Use no sustaining pedal except where indicated.

Lyric Piece (No. 16)

As might be guessed of music titled "Lyric Piece," it is primarily about song-like melody. The right-hand melody should predominate over the left-hand accompaniment in measures 3–12. The melody moves to the left hand in measures 12–17, before returning to the right hand in measure 17. Notice the phrasing that Kabalevsky has composed to shape the melody. The melancholy spirit, combined with the long melody, is reminiscent of Chopin. The composer takes the music into unexpected harmony in measure 17, then again in measure 21.

The Chase (No. 21)

This piece, with hands in octaves throughout, creates a brilliant and exciting impact. When well played it sounds harder than it actually is, because the music lies so easily under the hands. Pay attention to Kabalevsky's slurs, staccato and accents. The composer would have written in pedaling had he intended it. Use no pedal.

Novelette (No. 25)

The title "Novelette" was originally invented by Schumann (his Op. 21) for pensive, solemn music that tells a melancholy story. Kabalevsky intends that the sustaining pedal should be changed on each downbeat.

Slow Waltz from *24 Pieces for Children,* Op. 39 (No. 23) (composed 1944)

The *24 Pieces for Children* (alternately titled *24 Easy Pieces*) of Op. 39 are for an earlier level of study than Op. 27. Though Kabalevsky composed operas, orchestral music, concertos and chamber music throughout his career, as well as more difficult piano literature, he returned to writing music for piano students periodically in his life, reflecting his deeply felt commitment to music education. "Slow Waltz" echoes the spirit of a simple, melancholy waltz by Chopin. Notice how it is composed to allow *più mosso* (more movement, or a little faster) in measures 8–24, with the hand positions not jumping around in the left hand in this section.

Rondo-Toccata from *Four Rondos,* Op. 60 (No. 4) (composed 1958)

The piece can create a brilliant impact in performance. Because the left hand remains in a contained position through much of it, it will sound more difficult than it is. Note the change of touch, moving from staccato to legato in measure 17.

ARAM KHACHATURIAN
(1903–1978, Soviet/Armenian)

Aram Khachaturian was a seminal figure in 20th century Armenian and Soviet culture. Beloved in his homeland for bringing Armenia to prominence within the realm of Western art music, a major concert hall in Armenia's capital Yerevan bears his name, as well as a string quartet and an international competition for piano and composition. Born in Tbilisi, Georgia, of Armenian heritage, he grew up listening to Armenian folk songs but was also exposed to classical music early on through the Tbilisi's chapter of the Russian Music Society, the city's Italian Opera Theater, and visits by musicians such as Sergei Rachmaninoff. He moved to Moscow to study composition in 1921. Khachaturian's musical language combined Armenian folk influences with the Russian romantic tradition, embodying the official Soviet arts policy. He used traditional forms, such as theme and variations, sonata form, and Baroque suite forms, in creative ways, juxtaposing them with Armenian melodies and religious songs, folk dance rhythms, and a harmonic language that took inspiration from folk instruments such as the saz. He wrote symphonies, instrumental concertos, sonatas, ballets, and was the first Armenian composer to write film music. Khachaturian's most recognizable composition to the general public is "Sabre Dance" from the ballet *Gayane*. Starting in 1950, he also became active as an internationally touring conductor. He was awarded the Order of Lenin in 1939 and the Hero of Socialist Labor in 1973.

Ivan Sings from *Adventures of Ivan*
(composition begun 1926, completed 1947)
Khachaturian composed two albums for children. The first, completed in 1947, included *Adventures of Ivan*. The right hand is the singing (*cantabile*), rather poignant melody throughout; the left hand is an accompaniment to this melody. The composer makes it expressive with dynamics, crescendos, decrescendos, slurs, and specific uses of the sustaining pedal.

JOHANN PHILIPP KIRNBERGER
(1721–1783, German)

A student of J. S. Bach, Kirnberger was a life-long champion of the great composer, spending much of his life accumulating and ensuring the continued publication of Bach's music. Apart from composition, Kirnberger was also a theorist, inventing several alternate methods of tempering the tuning of a keyboard instrument. He held several court and church appointments throughout Germany and Poland, including the Chapel of Prince Heinrich of Prussia and Princess Anna Amalia.

The Chimes (Les Carillons)
This happy piece is in two large sections with the first section repeated, requiring a lightness of touch, crisp articulation, and steadiness in playing. It requires a refined, elegant tone and clarity from the pianist. Thus, do not use pedal. Notice that we have suggested playing the quarter notes detached. *Legato* touch is only applied in short slurred phrases of a few notes. In the *da capo* do not play the repeats of measures 1–8 or measures 8–20.

THEODOR KULLAK
(1818–1882, Prussian/German)

One of the most influential piano teachers of the nineteenth century, Kullak began giving concerts at age eight, with the official support of the royal family of Prussia, and met with enthusiastic reception when performing for other royal courts. After briefly studying medicine in Berlin he moved to Vienna, where he studied with Carl Czerny. At the age of 25, he began to work for the Prussian court as a music instructor, and specialized in teaching royal children and youth for many years. He co-founded what would become known as the Stern Conservatory in Berlin, as well as the Neue Akademie der Tonkunst, which became the largest private music school in the country. Through this school Kullak directly influenced thousands of pianists, including Hans Bischoff, Moritz Moszkowski, Xaver Scharwenka, and Nikolai Rubenstein. Writing almost exclusively for the piano, Kullak produced over 150 works, most of which were for students.

On the Playground (Spielchen auf der Wiese) from *Scenes from Childhood (Kinderleben I)*, Op. 62 (No. 4) (composed c. 1850)
Nothing but happy times occur on this playground. Playfulness in music is communicated by clear articulation and intention. A common type of play is to twirl, and the first phrase of the piece is like a child having fun twirling, first quickly and then slowing, eventually coming to a stop. The only held note, in measure 3, might mean that moment to recover from dizziness.

Grandmother Tells a Ghost Story (Grossmutter erzählt eine schauerliche Geschichte) from *Scenes from Childhood (Kinderleben II)*, Op. 81 (No. 3) (composed c. 1853)
A loving Grandmother tells a ghost story with a wink in her eye so that the children know that there is something fun going on. This playfulness is communicated with careful articulation and dynamics. The composer seems to have a narrative in mind. Why else would there be the f held note in measure 36, or in measure 44? The composer's wit comes through when he tells us as the music trails off in measure 54 that grandmother has fallen asleep. (This is Kullak's comment in the score.) After she falls asleep, the children know the story so well, having heard it many times before, that they finish it for her.

EDWARD MacDOWELL
(1860–1908, American)

Edward MacDowell showed talent at the piano from an early age. At 16 his mother took him to France to study at the Conservatoire de Paris. He continued his studies in Germany, where he met and performed for Franz Liszt, who encouraged the young composer. MacDowell married and in 1888 returned to the United States, settling in Boston. In 1896, the year *Woodland Sketches* was composed, he became professor of composition at Columbia University in New York. MacDowell was fundamental in building the music program at the school. He retired in 1904 following a buggy accident that gradually reduced his mental and physical health until his death. The MacDowell Colony in Petersburg, New Hampshire, was established in his honor for artists to find inspiration and solitude. MacDowell is often cited as the first American composer to gain stature and success in the European dominated classical music of his era.

To a Wild Rose from *Woodland Sketches*, Op. 51 (No. 1) (composed 1896)
Imagine taking a walk and coming upon a single, perfect wild rose. Such a discovery makes one stop in wonder. The piece is a long gaze at that delicate flower. It is essentially a song, with a melody in the top note of the right hand. Occasionally the left hand briefly answers the melody, such as in measure 14, or in measures 21 and 23. The composer only takes the player to f once and it is only briefly in measure 25.

WOLFGANG AMADEUS MOZART
(1756–1791, Austrian)

One of the most astonishing talents in the history of music, Mozart was first a child prodigy as a composer, keyboard player and violinist. He developed into a composer unrivalled by any, with a vast output in opera, symphonies, choral music, keyboard music and chamber music, all accomplished before his death at the young age of 35. Mozart spent most of his adult life living and working in Vienna. He was at the end of the era when successful musicians and composers attained substantial royal court appointments. A major position of this sort eluded him, despite his enormous talent, and he constantly sought opportunities to compose and perform. His music embodies the eighteenth century "age of reason" in its refined qualities, but adds playfulness, earnestness, sophistication and a deep sense of melody and harmony. Mozart's piano sonatas, concertos, sets of variations, and many other pieces at all levels from quite easy to virtuoso have become standards in the literature. His first compositions as a boy, from age five, were for keyboard. The notes on the individual pieces below were adapted from material previously published in *Mozart: 15 Intermediate Piano Pieces* (Schirmer Performance Editions).

Piece for Clavier in F Major, KV 33B (composed 1766)
Mozart composed this piece in October of 1766 on the back of minutes for a meeting of the Zurich Collegium Musicum, which indicates that the ten-year-old boy genius might have been bored during some formality. He likely performed it in Zurich on October 6 and 9, 1766. This happy music requires a light, bouncing touch in the broken octaves in the left hand. Play the left hand with light separation. Notice the recommended articulation for the right-hand melody. This piece should be played with no pedal.

Andantino in E-flat Major, KV 236 (588b)
(composed 1783?)
This piece is Mozart's adaptation of "Non vi turbate," an aria from Christoph Willibald Gluck's opera *Alceste*. Mozart may have heard this aria in a performance of the opera given at Schönbrunn Castle in Vienna on December 3, 1781. Mozart's keyboard piece was probably written in 1783, possibly as a theme upon which variations would be based, though this has not been conclusively proven. Mozart's adaptation is in AB form, with repeats, and concentrates primarily on the Gluck's orchestral introduction and conclusion to the aria.

Rondo in C Major, KV 334 (320b) (composed 1780)
This happy rondo is a keyboard arrangement, probably written by Mozart in the summer of 1780, of a movement from the composer's Divertimento in D Major for strings and horns. The piece is a simple rondo in ABABA form. Editorial suggestions have been made in the articulations to imitate the orchestration of the original music. Notice how Mozart playfully varies the theme when it recurs. Suggested sudden dynamic changes, appropriate to the period, will help make the music interesting.

Adagio for Glass Harmonica, KV 356 (617a)
(composed 1791)
This haunting piece was written in early 1791 for Marianne Krichgeßner, the nearly blind glass harmonica player who gave the first performance of a version for glass harmonica, flute, oboe, violin, and cello on August 19, 1791 in Vienna. The glass harmonica uses a series of glass bowls or goblets to produce musical tones through friction. The ethereal ringing sound produced is similar to when a finger rubs the moistened rim of a drinking glass. (Benjamin Franklin invented a version of the glass harmonica in 1757, which he called an armonica.) While the glass harmonica was something of a novelty instrument, this earnest and touching composition for it, with its poignantly rich harmonic changes, is certainly not a novelty piece at all.

Funeral March for Signor Maestro Contrapunto, KV 453a (composed 1784)
The march was composed in 1784 for Barbara Ployer, one of Mozart's students, to whom he also dedicated his Piano Concerto in E-flat Major, K. 449 and his Piano Concerto in G Major, K. 453. Maestro Contrapunto means Master Counterpoint. Counterpoint, meaning the combination of two or more melodic lines, reached its compositional zenith during the Baroque period. Its profuse use fell out of favor as the *stile galante* movement took hold during the mid-eighteenth century, and simpler, leaner music became more widespread. Barbara Ployer also took lessons from Mozart in music theory. This march, which lacks any counterpoint itself, is a musical joke raised as a result of Ployer's theory lessons. Performing this march, which is very dramatic with many *subito* changes in dynamics, requires a solemn-faced solemnity similar to an actor playing a very serious (and ultimately very ironic) role in a comedy.

German Dance in C Major, KV 605, No. 3
(composed 1791)
This piece is an arrangement, possibly by the composer himself, of one of the three German dances Mozart wrote for orchestra early in 1791, the last year of his life. In the original version for orchestra, Mozart introduces sleigh bells in the trio section (thus the name "The Sleighride" for this section).

ROBERT MUCZYNSKI
(1929–2010, American)

Composer and pianist Robert Muczynski studied at DePaul University in his hometown of Chicago with Alexander Tcherepnin. A brilliant pianist, at twenty-nine he made his Carnegie Hall debut with a performance of his own compositions. In addition to solo piano works, Muczynski mainly wrote for small chamber ensembles and also composed several orchestral pieces. His flute and saxophone sonatas, as well as *Time Pieces* for clarinet and piano, have become part of the standard repertoire for those instruments. In 1981, his concerto for saxophone was nominated for the Pulitzer Prize. Muczynski was composer in residence on the faculty of the University of Arizona from 1965 until his retirement in 1988.

Fable No. 9 from *Fables,* Op. 21 (composed 1965)

This set is subtitled "Nine Pieces for the Young," and was written for an eight-year-old piano student. Each of the fables has a distinct character. Muczynski was an excellent pianist, and his understanding of the instrument is evident in these compositions. About *Fables* the composer stated, "Few people realize how difficult it is to compose a piece that stays within the restrictions of that level. You have to restrain yourself when it comes to key choice, rhythmic complexity, and range. In *Fables* I tried to use strong patterns with the idea of liberating one hand by assigning it a repeating rhythmic or melodic figure."[1] The composer's metronome indication of a full 5/8 measure = 52 is extremely fast. If this cannot be attained, play at the fastest tempo that can be managed.

[1] From the preface to *Robert Muczynski: Collected Piano Pieces,* G. Schirmer, 1990.

CARL NIELSEN
(1865–1931, Danish)

Trained as a violinist from an early age, Nielsen entered the Copenhagen Conservatory in 1884, where he continued the study of the violin as well as composition. After graduation he performed as a freelance musician until he was able to secure a position in the second violin section of the Royal Theatre orchestra, one he would hold for sixteen years. On a tour of Europe he met and married Anne Marie Brodersen, a sculptor of some renown. The couple settled in Copenhagen in 1891, where both artists were able to work. Nielsen continued to compose, played in Royal Theatre orchestra, and occasionally conducted. His steady publishing of works eventually earned him a post at the Copenhagen Conservatory teaching theory, composition, and violin. His fame grew throughout his life. He became especially well-known outside Denmark after his death for his symphonic works, though he wrote in nearly every genre, including short piano pieces in a folk style.

Folk Melody (Im Volkston) from *Five Piano Pieces (Fünf Klavierstücke)*, Op. 3 (No. 1) (composed 1890)

Much of folk music is strophic, a term that means different words are sung over the same melody in succeeding verses. Nielsen takes a strophic approach to this folk melody. The song seems to be presented in its entirety through measure 12. Measures 13–20 are a repetition of measures 5–12, except for the addition of an imitative tenor voice that answers in canon. At measure 21 the composer returns to the music of the opening. Measure 25 is a *coda*, moving to the parallel major key. This piece might be an original composition imitating a folk style, or it might be composition based on an actual folk melody. The composer indicates that the beginning should be "like a hum," conjuring the thought of singing.

PIETRO DOMENICO PARADIES [PARADISI]
(1707–1791, Italian)

Paradisi (his original name) spent many unsuccessful years in Italy, attempting to establish himself as an opera composer. Failed stage works in Naples and Venice caused him to seek employment in London, where he changed his name to Paradies, as a teacher and composer of harpsichord music. He later moved back to Italy to retire. Though his vocal works never gained the notoriety he wished, his *Twelve Sonatas for Gravicembalo* (a predecessor to the piano) became extremely popular during his life and into the next century. The second movement of the sixth sonata is a perennial favorite of student pianists today, often published separately as "Toccata."

Toccata from Sonata No. 6 in A Major
(published in 1754)

A toccata is a brilliant composition showing virtuoso playing. This toccata is driven by relentless sixteenth notes. The greatest challenge is to master steadiness and evenness from start to finish. The eighth notes of the left hand, primarily, should be played detached throughout. The composer wrote no dynamics. Except for *mf* at the beginning we have not made editorial dynamics suggestions.

OCTAVIO PINTO
(1890–1950, Brazilian)

Octavio Pinto was born in Sao Paulo, Brazil, and enjoyed a successful career as an architect, but he was also an avid music lover, a skillful composer and pianist, and was well-connected to musical life in Brazil. In 1922 he married the famous piano virtuoso Gulomar Novaes, and he was also a close friend of composer Heitor Villa-Lobos. He took lessons for a time from Isidore Philipp, but it was mostly as a composer that his love and talent for music expressed itself throughout his life. He composed piano music, generally character pieces in nature or showpieces, until his death. His most well-known and oft-played work is *Scenas Infantis* (Memories of Childhood) of 1932, which became a signature piece performed by Novaes.

Playing Marbles (Bolinhas de vidro) from *Children's Festival (Festa de crianças): Little Suite for the Piano* (composed 1939)

This music requires a light touch throughout to achieve the composer's indication of *staccatissimo*. Alternating fingers on repeated notes (measures 5–6, 13–14, 17–20) is classic piano technique. Many student pianists encountering this piece may never have played a glissando. With your right hand rolled away from you and turned upside down, rest the fingernail of the third finger on the B natural note where the glissando begins. Using your fingernail only, slide it over the white keys until you reach beat one of the next measure, and strike this note conventionally with the same finger. Be careful not to use the knuckle, as this can hurt and cause bleeding.

SERGEI PROKOFIEV
(1891–1953, Russian)

Russian composer and pianist Sergei Prokofiev pushed the boundaries of Russian romanticism without fully disregarding its influence. Influenced by the formal aspects of works by Haydn and Mozart, he was also a pioneering neo-classicist. Prokofiev was born in eastern Ukraine, but travelled often with his mother to Moscow and St. Petersburg where he was exposed to works such as Gounod's *Faust*, Borodin's *Prince Igor*, Tchaikovsky's *Sleeping Beauty*, and operas such as *La Traviata* and *Carmen*. His prodigious musical abilities as a child led him to lessons with Reinhold Glière and then studies at the St. Petersburg Conservatory. He composed several sonatas and symphonies during his studies, as well as his first piano concerto, which he played for his piano exam at the conservatory, taking first prize. In 1917, following the October Revolution, he left Russia, first moving to the United States and then settling in Europe. He continued to tour internationally after returning to the Soviet Union in 1936, until the authorities confiscated his passport two years later. During World War II Prokofiev was evacuated from the USSR. It was a difficult time for composers and artists in Soviet Russia. Between 1946 and '48, Soviet political leader Andrey Zhdanov passed a number of resolutions with the intent of heavily regulating artistic output and keeping it in line with the ideals of socialist realism and the Communist Party.

Selections from *Music for Children*, Op. 65
(composed 1935)
In the midst of many months of work on the large ballet *Romeo and Juliet*, a commission from the Kirov Ballet, Prokofiev refreshed his creativity briefly by shifting his focus to composing the twelve piano miniatures comprising *Music for Children*, Op. 65.

Morning (No. 1)
One of the implied topics that Prokofiev is teaching in this piece is the need for a graceful shift of hand position into different ranges of the piano, including the crossing of hands. These hand position shifts need to be anticipated and played with elegance. Though the music is full of colorful features and figures, it is contained in volume and quiet in spirit. Measure 23 needs to be played very gracefully or the notes will sound "wrong."

Promenade (No. 2)
The composer's implication for the left-hand quarter notes in measures 1–20 without articulation markings is that these should be played with slight separation. If he had intended legato playing, he would have indicated this. This *Allegretto* should not be played too quickly.

Regrets (No. 5)
Prokofiev's ability to make such a strong emotional statement in such a brief piece reminds one of Schumann. The priorities are: tone, phrasing, dynamics, careful pedaling, and in general, sensitive musicality. Notice the specific notes that Prokofiev has marked with the stress or tenuto marking. The "hairpin" rise and fall in volume also implies phrasing. Notice the "comma" (meaning a brief and graceful lift of the hands) at the end of measure 16 before moving to the *tranquillo* middle section. The composer decorates the melody with variations upon its return in measure 25. The surprising change of harmony and content at measure 37 is marked with **pp**, which can be magical.

JEAN-PHILIPPE RAMEAU
(1683–1764, French)

Rameau studied with his father, an organist, before continuing his music education in Italy. He returned to France as a violinist in a traveling music troupe and then became organist at Clermont Cathedral. By 1706, Rameau was in Paris serving in various places as organist and publishing his first keyboard works. After a few brief appointments as organist in Dijon and Lyons, Rameau returned to Paris permanently. He published his most famous theoretical work, *Traité de l'harmonie*, in 1722. Late in life, the composer took up writing operas. Rameau is remembered as one of the most influential composers of keyboard music of the French Baroque.

Tambourin from *Pièces de clavecin* (*Harpsichord Pieces*), (published in 1724, revised in 1731)
A tambourin is a drum from the Provence region of France. In the eighteenth century, a French dance invented for the theatre was based on this drum. A tambourin has bass notes that are pedal tones (the E-minor harmony in this piece), an oboe-like melody and duple meter. The composer gave no tempo indication. We have suggested *moderato*, which allows for a wide range of choices. Note that the trills begin on the note above. The composer provided no articulation or dynamics. We have made articulation suggestions that reflect the French Baroque style. Dynamics are much more subjective and there are many possibilities. We recommend using no pedal in this piece.

MAURICE RAVEL
(1875–1937, French)

Ravel was born in Ciboure, a Basque villa in the southwestern corner of France to Swiss and Basque parents, but raised in Paris, his lifelong use of exotic influences in his music stemmed from his heritage-based affinity for Basque and Spanish culture. Ravel studied piano and then composition with Gabriel Fauré at the Paris Conservatoire, though he was dismissed for not meeting the necessary requirements in either piano or composition. This, along with his heritage, may have influenced the lack of support he received from French music critics and the Société Nationale de Musique, Paris' leading concert society. Critics often pitted him unfavorably against Debussy and accused him of copying Debussy's style. In 1909, Ravel founded the Société Musicale Indépendente in opposition to the Société

Nationale, naming Fauré president. This society strove to organize performances of both French and foreign works regardless of their style or genre. The same year Ravel wrote *Daphnis et Chloé* for famed choreographer Diaghilev and began his close friendship with Igor Stravinsky. He joined the army as a driver in the motor transport corps during World War I, a tragic time in which he was also deeply affected by the loss of his mother, with whom he was extremely close. He lived the rest of his life thirty miles west of Paris in Montfort-l'Amaury surrounded by the Forest of Rambouillet, travelling around Europe and North America performing and attending premieres of his works.

Prélude (composed 1913)

French style in the Impressionist period requires sophistication of touch, phrasing, pedaling and musicality. This little known Prélude is about elegant, languorous phrase and lush harmony. Pay careful attention to Ravel's phrase markings. The rolled chord in the right hand in measure 16 and 18 will take some practice for most hands. If your hand is too small to hold all the notes down after they are rolled, then experiment with letting one or two of the notes go, sustaining the sound with careful use of the sustaining pedal, keeping the harmonies clear.

MAX REGER
(1873–1916, German)

Reger's father, an amateur musician of some talent, was the boy's first teacher. Soon Max was studying piano and organ privately, and by the age of sixteen was playing organ for church services. Composer Hugo Riemann became aware of Reger's compositional talents. Reger was Riemann's student and followed him to the conservatory in Wiesbaden. After completing his education he served the required year of military service before teaching privately and composing. Reger moved to Munich in 1901, continuing to compose, concertize as a pianist, and teach, until he was offered a position at the Munich Akademie der Tonkunst. In 1907 Reger became the director of music at the University of Leipzig, and subsequently professor of composition, a post he held until his death. Adding to his list of responsibilities, Reger accepted a court position in Meiningen. This rigorous schedule, along with an alleged life-long struggle with alcoholism, led to a premature death. The *Album for Young People*, Op. 17 *(Aus der Jugendzeit)* was composed in 1895.

The Dead Little Bird (Das tote Vöglein)
from *Album for Young People (Aus der Jugendzeit)*,
Op. 17 (No. 4) (composed 1895)

Max Reger's music has chromaticism characteristic of German Romantic composers of the late nineteenth century into the early twentieth century. The harmony oozes along with wonderfully colorful and surprising changes. It is obviously a sad event for a child to come upon a dead bird. This music captures the empathy and reverence in that sadness, as well as a sense of somber wonder at death. Even though the notes are quite simple, this composition asks for mature musicality from the pianist to build beautifully constructed phrases.

DOMENICO SCARLATTI
(1685–1757, Italian)

Domenico was one of two musical sons of composer Alessandro Scarlatti. Domenico was extraordinarily influential in the development of solo keyboard music, composing nearly 600 sonatas for the instrument. He was taught by his father and other musicians in Naples until he secured the position of composer and organist for the royal chapel in Naples at the age of 15. He spent time in Venice and Rome serving as the Maestro di cappella at St. Peter's before moving to Lisbon, where he taught the Portuguese Princess. In 1728, he moved to Spain where he would spend the rest of his life, finally settling in Madrid, where he was the music master for the Princess and later Queen of Spain. A sonata in the Baroque period is different from its mature development in the Classical era. A sonata in the Italian Baroque almost always meant a one-movement instrumental piece. Its musical form was not defined and could be many possibilities. The Italian Baroque style is distinctly different from the German Baroque style and the French Baroque style. Without going into complicated detail, the Italian Baroque style had more freedom than its German counterpart. These are some of the easiest of Scarlatti's sonatas.

Sonata in G Major, L. 79 (K. 391, P. 364)
(composition date unknown)

Our editorial suggestions for articulation indicate some stylistic qualities of the period. Scarlatti's music often has a playful quality, and we have indicated dynamics which differ upon repeated sections to help create this playfulness. Trills begin on the note above in this period. The *acciaccatura*, which appears on the downbeat of measure 11, is to be played quickly with the principle note on the beat. No pedal should be used.

Sonata in D minor, L. 423 (K. 32, P. 14)
(composition date unknown)

This aria, closely related to vocal music, has a typical quality of Baroque melancholy. The thirty-second notes which appear many places are written out ornaments in this edition. We have made stylistic suggestions about which notes should be slurred (meaning that the notes in the slurred group are played *legato*) and which should be played *staccato*. The short two-note and three-note slurs are a typical Baroque musical indication of weeping.

ROBERT SCHUMANN
(1810–1856, German)

One of the principal composers of the Romantic era, Robert Schumann's relatively short creative career gave the world major repertoire in symphonies, art song, chamber music and piano music. Besides being a composer, Schumann was an accomplished writer about music, especially as a critic then editor of the influential *Neue Zeitschrift für Musik*. He was married to concert pianist Clara Wieck, who championed his works after his death in 1856, the result a severe struggle with mental illness. Schumann was an early supporter of the young Johannes Brahms. *Scenes from Childhood*, Op. 15 (*Kinderszenen*) was likely composed in February of 1838. Schumann originally composed thirty pieces for the set, but discarded many in reaching his final choice of thirteen pieces. These are adult reminiscences of childhood. The *Album for the Young* (*Album für die Jugend*), a collection of 43 short piano pieces, composed in 1838 for Schumann's three daughters. Schumann made a specialty of short character pieces for piano, not entirely unrelated to his distinctive work as a major composer of art song.

Of Strange Lands and People (Von fremden Ländern und Menshcen) from *Scenes from Childhood* (*Kinderszenen*), Op. 15 (No. 1) (composed 1838)

One of Schumann's most famous piano pieces, the title "Of Strange Lands and People" implies dreamy imagination of places far away. The music is constructed in three voices. The treble melody is the top note in the right hand. (This voice is supported by an alto harmony underneath it in measures 9–12.) The second voice is the bass line, single notes throughout, the lowest note in the writing. The third voice is that of the moving triplets. There also is an implied fourth voice, which is the first note of the triplet figure in measures 1–8 and measure 15 to the end. The composer apparently gave this piece no tempo marking. Too often, one hears a student pianist play this piece too quickly and too loudly, destroying its wistful dreaminess.

Hunting Song (Jägerliedchen) from *Album for the Young* (*Album für die Jugend*), Op. 68 (No. 7) (composed 1848)

Schumann's piece captures the high spirits of a hunting party, echoing the bugle calls and conjuring the horse's gallop. Even though Schumann did not give us a different dynamic for the staccato phrase, he restates the *f* after it, which implies that the pianist should probably lighten up for the staccato notes. Some pianists might find it easier in measures 18 and 20 to play the alto voice E in the left hand, so that the right hand is only playing single notes. In this edition, we have indicated pedaling in three spots only. The playful quality of the hunt also comes through in the sharp dynamic contrasts, moving at times from *ff* to *p*, back to *ff*, then *p*.

The Reaper's Song (Schnitterliedchen) from *Album for the Young* (*Album für die Jugend*), Op. 68 (No. 18) (composed 1848)

Swinging of the scythe is field work that has a rhythm about it, and Schumann captures the spirit of that work with rhythm in 6/8 meter. He also adds a folk-like quality by adding the double pedal tone at the beginning. This reaper seems to be quite happy at work, and he or she does it with a light touch. Voicing is a paramount component of the "Reaper's Song." Notice Schumann's the two-measure

phrases in measures 1–2, 3–4, etc.; the phrase structure changes in measure 14, with phrases of four measures. The entire piece is to be played gently and softly except for the middle section, which is marked *f*. The texture changes for the final section, beginning in measure 29, with staccato markings, the first encountered in this piece.

Little Romance (Kleine Romanze) from *Album for the Young* (*Album für die Jugend*), Op. 68 (No. 19) (composed 1848)

This "Little Romance" is quite similar to a melody that would be sung by a singer. We can only guess that Schumann had in mind a little romance that did not exactly end happily. One gets the impression that whatever has happened, sad as it might be at the moment, things will quickly move on. The piece should generally be played without pedal, with the fingers executing the *legato*, except for the few spots where pedal is suggested. Dynamic contrasts are quite important. It is common to feel dramatic sudden changes of emotion when dealing with romantic troubles.

DMITRI SHOSTAKOVICH
(1906–1975, Russian)

A major mid-twentieth century composer, Shostakovich is famous for his epic symphonies, concertos, operas, string quartets, and other chamber works. Born in St. Petersburg, his entire career took place in Soviet-era Russia. His life teetered between receiving high official honors and living with an almost debilitating fear of arrest for works that did not adhere to the Soviet ideals of socialist realism. In 1934, his opera *Lady Macbeth of the Mtsensk District* met with great popular success, but was banned by Stalin for the next thirty years as modernist, surrealist, and obscene. The following year, Stalin began a campaign known as the Purges, executing or exiling to prison camps politicians, intellectuals and artists. Shostakovich managed to avoid such a fate, and despite an atmosphere of anxiety and repression was able to compose an astounding number of works with originality, humor, and emotional power. He succeeded in striking a balance between modernism and tradition that continues to make his music accessible to a broad audience. An excellent pianist, Shostakovich performed concertos by Mozart, Prokofiev, and Tchaikovsky early in his career, but after 1930 limited himself to performing his own works and some chamber music. He taught instrumentation and composition at the Leningrad Conservatory from 1937–1968, with brief breaks due to war and other political disruptions, and at the Moscow Conservatory in the 1940s. Since his death in 1975, Shostakovich has become one of the most performed twentieth century composers.

Birthday from *Children's Notebook for Piano*, Op. 69 (No. 7) (composed 1944–45)

Among a huge output of symphonies, operas and chamber music, Shostakovich wrote only a few pieces for piano students. *Children's Notebook for Piano* was written for his eight-year-old daughter, Galina, for her studies on the instrument. The original set was published as six pieces. The seventh piece, "Birthday," written in celebration of Galina's ninth birthday in 1945, was added in a later edition. After the introduction "fanfare," the music settles into a rather languid waltz in measure 7. Shostakovich's composed articulations imply that he intended no sustaining pedal to be used in this piece.

PYOTR IL'YICH TCHAIKOVSKY
(1840–1893, Russian)

Tchaikovsky was the great Russian composer of the nineteenth century who achieved the most international success, and whose symphonies, ballets, operas, chamber music and piano music continue to be a central part of the repertoire. Of his piano works, *The Seasons*, Op. 37bis, *Album for the Young*, Op. 39 and his concerto are most familiar to present day pianists and teachers. *Album for the Young* was written in four days in May of 1878, with revisions later that year before publication in October. It was during this year that Tchaikovsky left his teaching post at the St. Petersburg Conservatory and began composing and conducting full time, a move made financially possible by the patronage of Nadezhda von Meck. Much of *Album for the Young* is inspired by folksongs, capturing observations and experiences from childhood in 24 fanciful miniatures.

The Wooden Soldier's March
from *Album for the Young*, Op. 39 (No. 5)
(composed 1878)
Notice that Tchaikovsky keeps this march of toy soldiers in the treble range of the piano, which is appropriate for these tiny figurines. This toy soldier's march is not far removed from the march in *The Nutcracker* by the same composer. There is no need for pedal in any part of this piece. The toy aspect is captured also by the soft dynamic that Tchaikovsky has given. (Small toys do not have enough size to create a louder presence.) The articulation that the composer has given us is a perfect map to create an effective performance. A brief military trumpet call occurs in measures 8, 16, and 40.

Mazurka in D minor from *Album for the Young*,
Op. 39 (No. 11) (composed 1878)
A mazurka is a Polish folk dance in triple meter, slower than a waltz, in which each beat is distinctly heard. Chopin developed the mazurka to a high art form. Tchaikovsky's piece is much simpler than a Chopin mazurka, and closer to the mazurka's folk roots. The accents that Tchaikovsky includes add to its dance-like, folk quality. Tchaikovsky's articulations and dynamics are precise and intricate, shifting suddenly at times.

Sweet Dream from *Album for the Young*,
Op. 39 (No. 21) (composed 1878)
In a Romantic period composition, when a composer states "with much feeling," it is an invitation to the performer to bring interpretation beyond what can be notated in the score. In other words, in this period it is simply not possible in music notation to write down all the details of expression which are part of the style. Nuances and phrase shape and very slight *rit.* here and there that help the piece come alive. This music is full of sincerity.

GEORG PHILIPP TELEMANN
(1681–1767, German)

A prominent German Baroque composer, Telemann was instrumental in expanding figured bass composition and defining Baroque ornamentation. He is sometimes cited as the most prolific composer who ever lived, with over 3,000 known music works, including about 150 keyboard pieces. He also wrote and published poetry. Telemann was a self-taught musician who held a series of positions in Leipzig, Sorau, Eisenach, Frankfurt, and finally Hamburg, where he became the music director of the city's churches.

Cantabile in F Major (composition date unknown)
The word cantabile means singing. In this case the composer means that the melody should be played with a singing tone. The left hand is the accompaniment that keeps the beat steady and disciplines the melody. The left hand quarter notes should be played slightly detached throughout. On top of this, the right hand achieves its expressiveness through thoughtful articulation.

—Richard Walters, editor

THE 18TH CENTURY

In Progressive Order of Difficulty

The pieces were previously published in the following Schirmer Performance Editions volumes.

Anonymous: Minuet in A minor, BWV Appendix 120
Anonymous: Polonaise in G minor, BWV Appendix 119
C.P.E. Bach: March in G Major, BWV Appendix 124
from *Selections from the Notebook for Anna Magdalena Bach*
edited by Christos Tsitsaros

Bourrée, BWV 996
from *First Lessons in Bach*
edited by Christos Tsitsaros

Prelude in D minor, BWV 926
Prelude in F Major, BWV 927
Prelude in C minor, BWV 999
from *J.S. Bach: Nineteen Little Preludes*
edited by Christos Tsitsaros

German Dance in G Major, WoO 8, No. 6
German Dance in C Major, WoO 8, No. 7
German Dance in B-flat Major, WoO 13, No. 2
from *Beethoven: Selected Piano Works*
edited by Matthew Edwards

Couperin: The Little Trifle
Dandrieu: Lament
Handel: Allegro from Suite in G minor, HWV 432
Handel: Prelude in G Major, HWV 442
Kirnberger: The Chimes
Paradies: Toccata from Sonata No. 6 in A Major
Rameau: Tambourin
Scarlattti: Sonata in G Major, L. 79
Scarlatti: Sonata in D minor, L. 423
Telemann: Cantabile in F Major
from *The Baroque Era: Intermediate Level*
edited by Richard Walters

C.P.E. Bach: Solfeggietto in C minor
Haydn: Allegro from Sonata in C Major, Hob. XVI/1
from *The Classical Era: Intermediate Level*
edited by Richard Walters

Adagio for Glass Harmonica, KV 356 (617a)
Andantino in E-flat Major, KV 236 (588b)
Funeral March for Signor Maestro Contrapunto, KV 453a
German Dance in C Major, KV 605, No. 3
Piece for Clavier in F Major, KV 33B
Rondo in C Major, KV 334 (320b)
from *Mozart: 15 Intermediate Piano Pieces*
edited by Elena Abend

Minuet in A minor

from The Notebook for Anna Magdalena Bach

Composer unknown
BWV Appendix 120

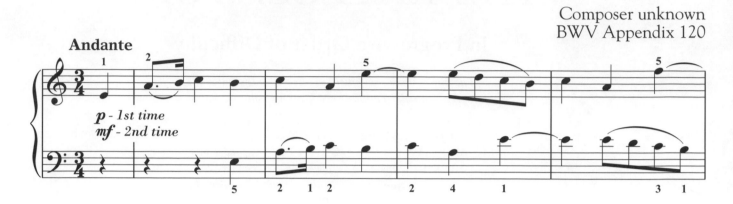

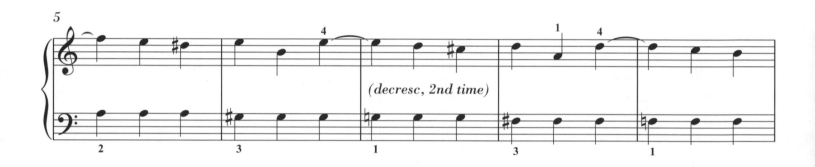

Fingering by Christos Tsitsaros.
Tempo, articulations, and dynamics are editorial suggestions.

March in G Major

from *The Notebook for Anna Magdalena Bach*

Carl Philipp Emanuel Bach
BWV Appendix 124

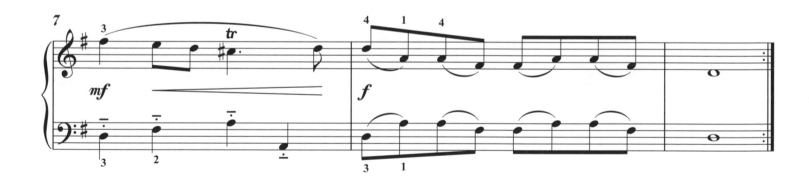

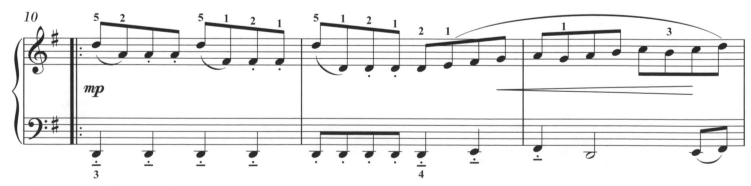

Fingering by Christos Tsitsaros.
Tempo, articulations, and dynamics are editorial suggestions.

Polonaise in G minor

from *The Notebook for Anna Magdalena Bach*

Composer unknown
BWV Appendix 119

Fingering by Christos Tsitsaros.
*These wedge markings in the right hand, indicating marcato, appear in the source manuscript. Other articulations, tempo and dynamics are editorial suggestions.

Sonata in D minor

Domenico Scarlatti
L. 423 (K. 32, P. 14)

Fingering by Jeannie Yu.
Tempo, articulations and dynamics are stylistic editorial suggestions. Ornaments have been realized for this edition.

Andantino in E-flat Major

Adaptation of an aria* by Christoph Willibald Gluck

Wolfgang Amadeus Mozart
KV 236 (588b)

* "Non vi turbate" from *Alceste*.
Edited and with fingering by Elena Abend.
Editorial suggestions are in brackets.

Funeral March for Signor Maestro Contrapunto

Wolfgang Amadeus Mozart
KV 453a

Edited and with fingering by Elena Abend.
Editorial suggestions are in brackets.

Piece for Clavier in F Major
(Klavierstück)

Wolfgang Amadeus Mozart
KV 33B

Edited and with fingering by Elena Abend.
Editorial suggestions are in brackets.

[*poco rit. 2nd time*]

German Dance in C Major

Ludwig van Beethoven
WoO 8, No. 7

Edited and with fingering by Matthew Edwards.
Editorial suggestions are in brackets.

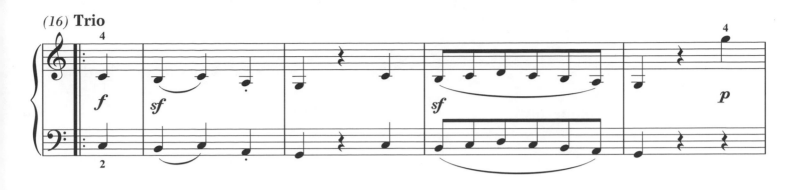

(16) **Trio**

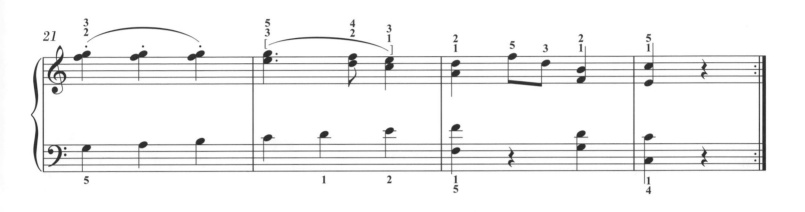

D.C. al Fine
senza repetizione

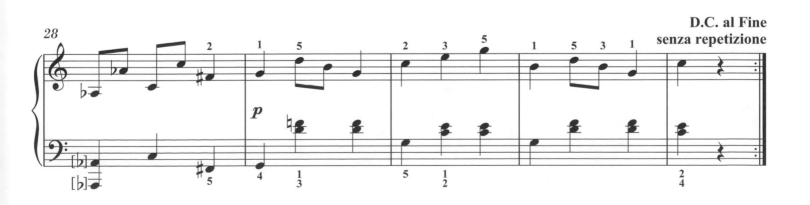

German Dance in B-flat Major

Ludwig van Beethoven
WoO 13, No. 2

[**Allegro moderato**]

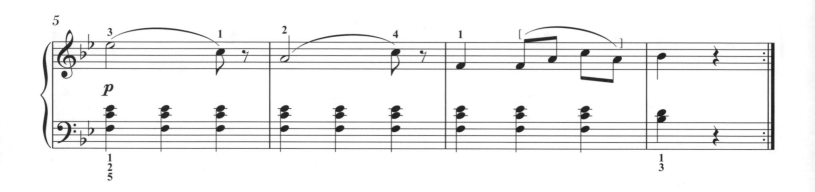

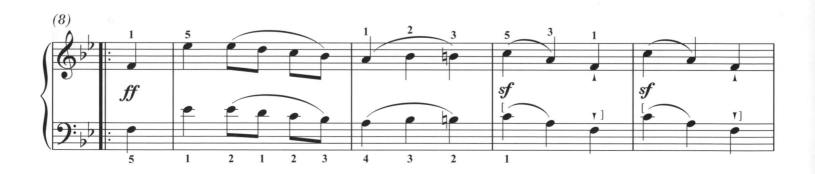

Edited and with fingering by Matthew Edwards.

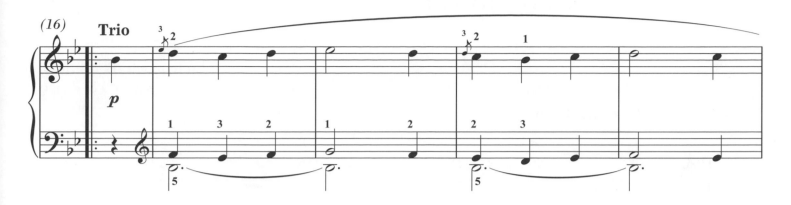

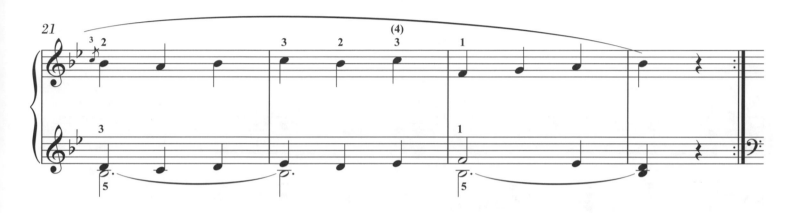

D.C. al Fine
senza repetizione

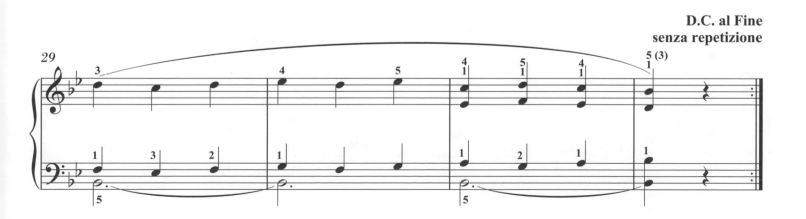

German Dance in G Major

Ludwig van Beethoven
WoO 8, No. 6

[**Allegro moderato**]

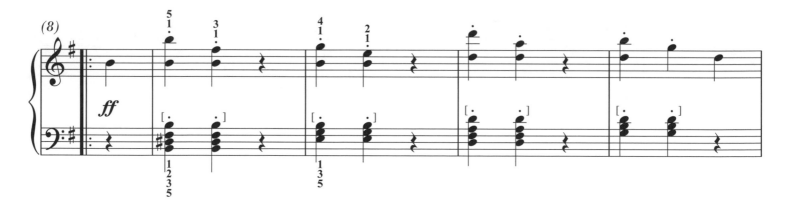

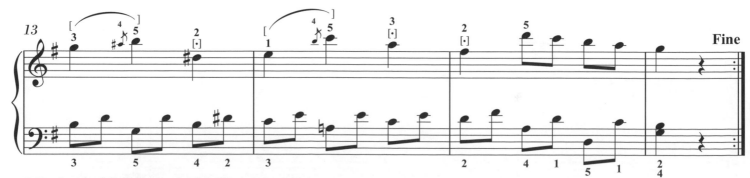

Edited and with fingering by Matthew Edwards.
Editorial suggestions are in brackets.

D.C. al Fine
senza repetizione

The Chimes
(Les Carillons)

Johann Philipp Kirnberger

Fingering by Stefanie Jacob.
Tempo, articulations and dynamics are stylistic editorial suggestions. Trills begin on the note above.
No repeats on the *Da Capo*.

ALTERNATIVO

Cantabile in F Major

Georg Philipp Telemann

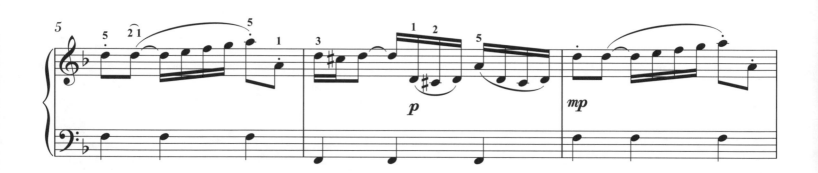

left hand quarter notes slightly detached throughout

Fingering by Elena Abend.
Tempo, articulations and dynamics are editorial suggestions.

German Dance in C Major

Wolfgang Amadeus Mozart
KV 605, No. 3

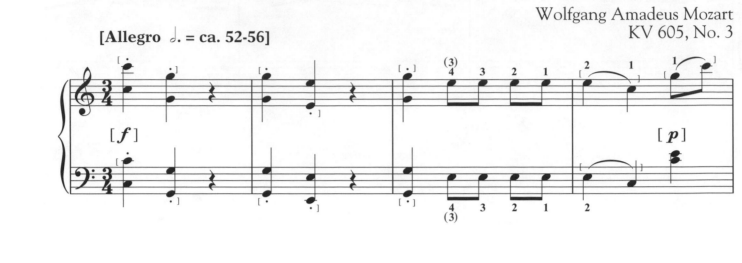

Eliminate repeats on the Da Capo.
Edited and with fingering by Elena Abend.
Editorial suggestions are in brackets.

Trio (The Sleighride)

D.C. al Fine
second time

Prelude in G Major

from *Suite de pièce*, Volume 2, No. 9

George Frideric Handel
HWV 442

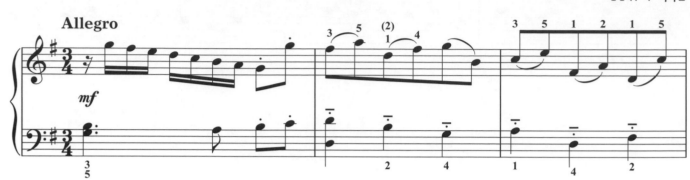

Fingering by Jeannie Yu.
Articulations and dynamics are stylistic editorial suggestions.

Adagio for Glass Harmonica

Wolfgang Amadeus Mozart
KV 356 (617a)

Edited and with fingering by Elena Abend.
Editorial suggestions are in brackets.

Bourrée
from Lute Suite No. 1 in E minor

Johann Sebastian Bach
BWV 996

[Allegro moderato]

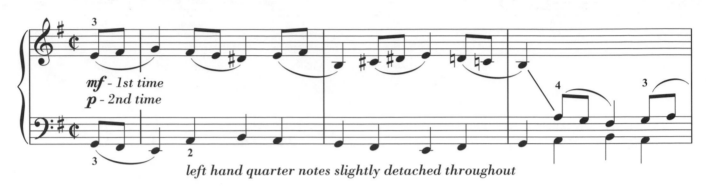

mf - 1st time
p - 2nd time

left hand quarter notes slightly detached throughout

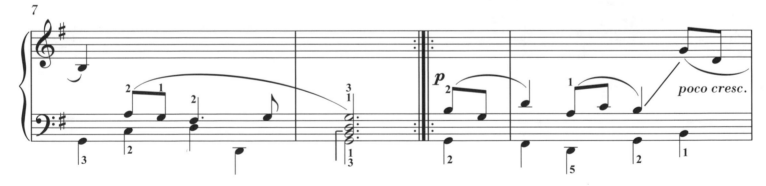

poco cresc.

p

Edited and with fingering by Christos Tsitsaros.
Tempo, articulations and dynamics are editorial suggestions. Bach indicated none of these details in his manuscript.

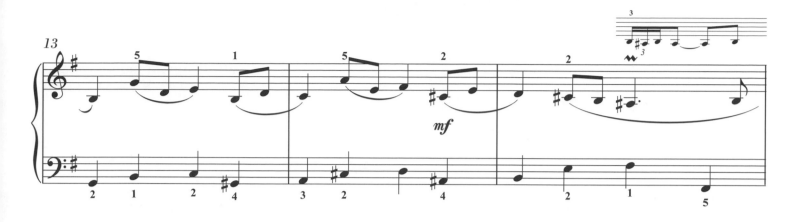

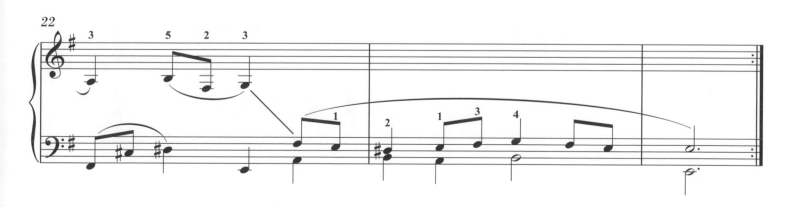

Rondo in C Major

Wolfgang Amadeus Mozart
KV 334 (320b)

Edited and with fingering by Elena Abend.
Editorial suggestions are in brackets.

Tambourin
from *Pièces de clavecin*

Jean-Philippe Rameau

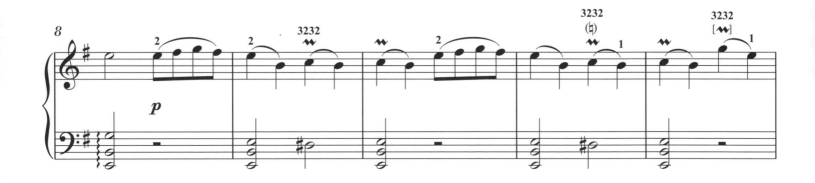

Fingering by Matthew Edwards.
Tempo, articulation and dynamics are stylistic editorial suggestions. Trills begin on the note above.

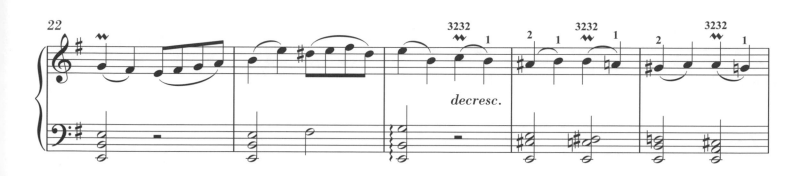

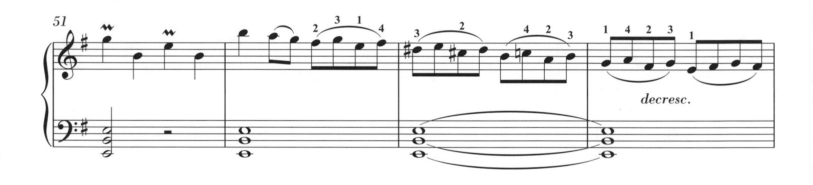

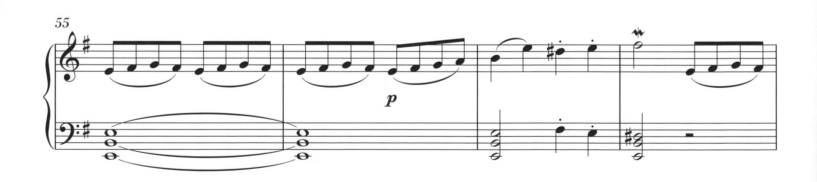

Lament
(La Gémissante)
from *Premier livre de pièces de clavecin*

Jean-François Dandrieu

Fingering by Elena Abend.

The ornamentation for this piece has been omitted for this édition. Tempo, dynamics and articulations are stylistic editorial suggestions. Trills begin on the note above. Repeat of the first section is optional in performance.

Allegro
from Sonata in C Major

Franz Joseph Haydn
Hob. XVI/1

Fingering by Stefanie Jacob.

Sonata in G Major

Domenico Scarlatti
L. 79 (K. 391, P. 364)

Fingering by Jeannie Yu.
Articulation and dynamics are stylistic editorial suggestions. Trills begin on the note above.

Prelude in C minor

Johann Sebastian Bach
BWV 999

[Allegro moderato]

Edited and with fingering by Christos Tsitsaros.
Editorial suggestions appear in brackets.

Allegro
from Suite in G minor

George Frideric Handel
HWV 432

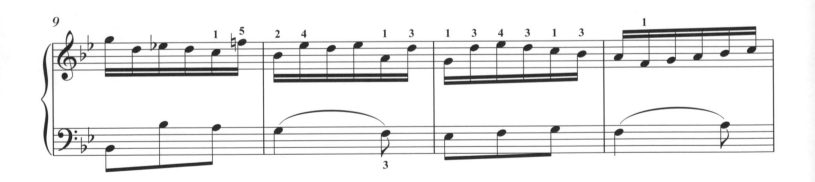

Fingering by Jeannie Yu.
Articulations and dynamics are stylistic editorial suggestions. Trills begin on the note above.

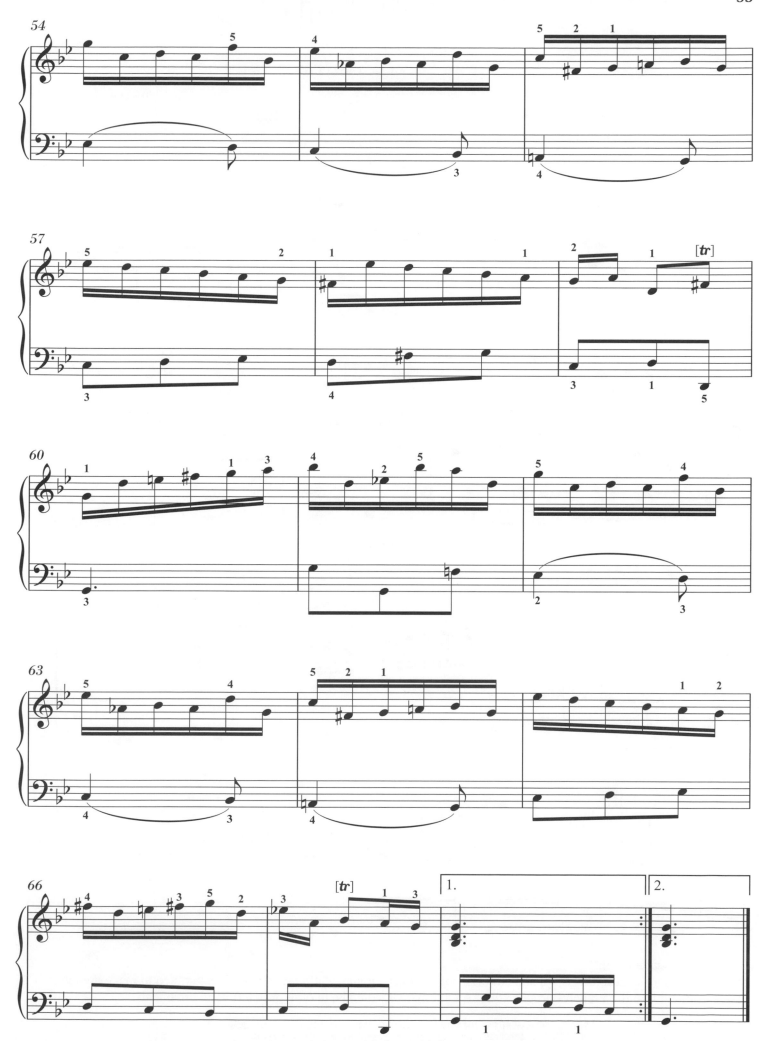

The Little Trifle

(Le Petit-Rien)
from *Pièces de clavecin*

François Couperin

Fingering by Jeannie Yu.
Dynamics and articulations are stylistic editorial suggestions. Ornamentation, which may be omitted to make the piece easier, is integral to the French Baroque style. An alternative would be to omit only left hand ornaments.

COUPLET 2

Solfeggietto in C minor

Carl Philipp Emanuel Bach
H. 220

Non troppo vivo

Fingering by Elena Abend.
Dynamics are editorial suggestions.

Prelude in D minor

Johann Sebastian Bach
BWV 926

Edited and with fingering by Christos Tsitsaros.
Editorial suggestions are in brackets.

Prelude in F Major

Johann Sebastian Bach
BWV 927

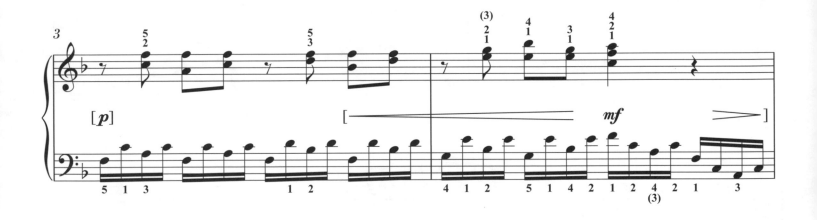

Edited and with fingering by Christos Tsitsaros.
Editorial suggestions are in brackets.

Toccata
from Sonata No. 6 in A Major

Pietro Domenico Paradies [Paradisi]

Fingering by Stefanie Jacob.
Tempo and dynamics are stylistic editorial suggestions. Play eighth notes, in right or left hand, slightly detached throughout.

THE 19TH CENTURY

In Progressive Order of Difficulty

The pieces were previously published in the following
Schirmer Performance Editions volumes.

Beach: Gavotte in D minor
Kullak: Grandmother Tells a Ghost Story
Kullak: On the Playground
MacDowell: To a Wild Rose
Nielsen: Folk Melody
Reger: The Dead Little Bird
from *The Romantic Era: Intermediate Level*
edited by Richard Walters

Gentle Complaint
Restlessness
from *Burgmüller: 25 Progressive Studies, Op. 100*
edited by Margaret Otwell

Confidence
from *Burgmüller: 18 Characteristic Studies, Op. 109*
edited by William Westney

Prelude in A Major
Prelude in B minor
Prelude in E minor
from *Chopin: Préludes, Op. 28*
edited by Brian Ganz

Arietta
Dance of the Elves
Puck
Waltz in A minor
from *Grieg: Selected Lyric Pieces*
edited by William Westney

Hunting Song
The Little Wanderer
from *Gurlitt: Albumleaves for the Young, Op. 101*
edited by Margaret Otwell

Study in A minor (The Avalanche)
from *Heller: Selected Piano Studies, Op. 45 & 46*
edited by William Westney

Hunting Song
Little Romance
Of Strange Lands and People
The Reaper's Song
from *Schumann: Selections from Album for the Young, Op. 68*
edited by Jennifer Linn

Mazurka in D minor
Sweet Dream
The Wooden Soldier's March
from *Tchaikovsky: Album for the Young. Op. 39*
edited by Alexandre Dossin

Gavotte in D minor
from *Children's Album*

Amy Marcy Beach
Op. 36, No. 2

Fingering is from the first edition.

The Reaper's Song
(Schnitterliedchen)
from *Album for the Young*

Robert Schumann
Op. 68, No. 18

Nicht sehr schnell
Not very fast

Edited and with fingering by Jennifer Linn.

To a Wild Rose
from *Woodland Sketches*

Edward MacDowell
Op. 51, No. 1

Fingering by Matthew Edwards.

Grandmother Tells a Ghost Story

from *Scenes from Childhood*
(Kinderleben II)

Theodor Kullak
Op. 81, No. 3

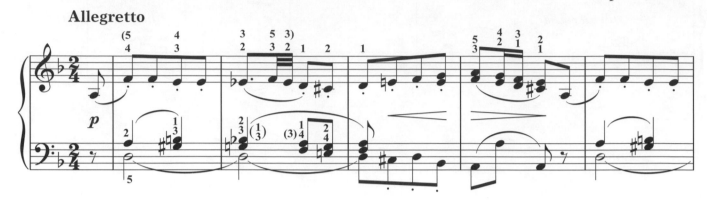

Fingering by Matthew Edwards.

On the Playground

from *Scenes from Childhood*
(Kinderleben I)

Theodor Kullak
Op. 62, No. 4

Allegro vivace

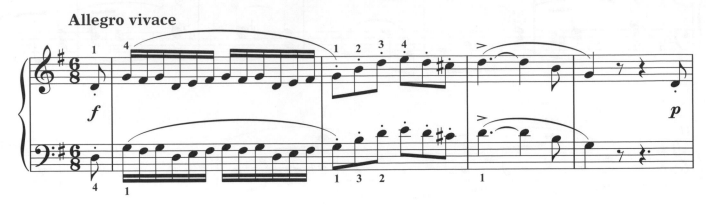

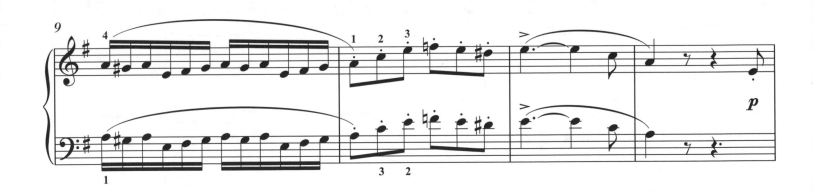

Fingering by Matthew Edwards.

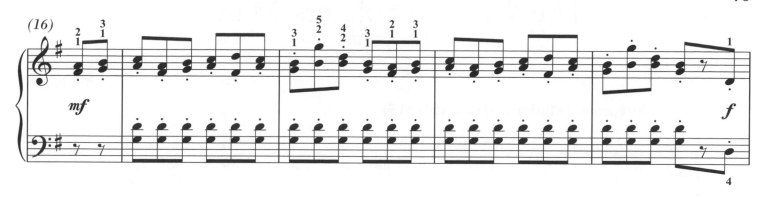

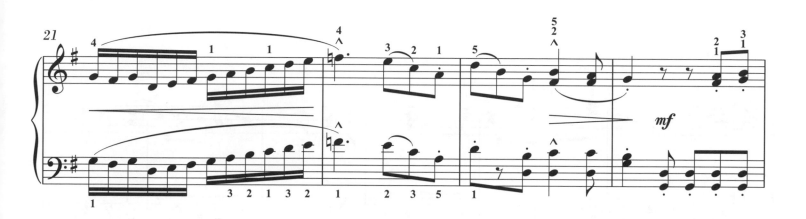

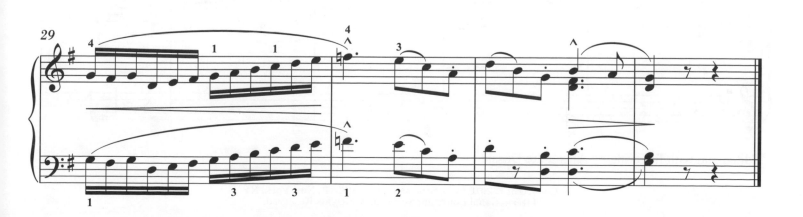

The Wooden Soldiers' March

from *Album for the Young*

Pyotr Il'yich Tchaikovsky
Op. 39, No. 5

Умеренно [Moderate] (♩ = 105–115)

Edited and with fingering by Alexandre Dossin.

Gentle Complaint

(Douce Plainte)

from *25 Progressive Studies*

(*25 Études faciles et progressive*)

Johann Friedrich Burgmüller
Op. 100, No. 16

Allegro moderato (♩ = 126)

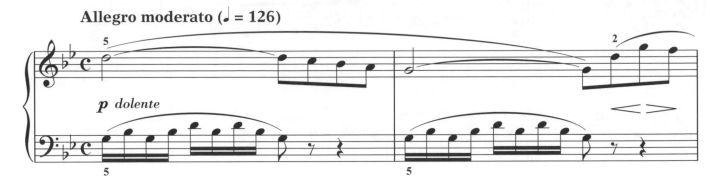

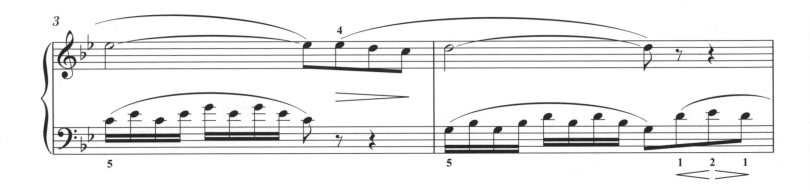

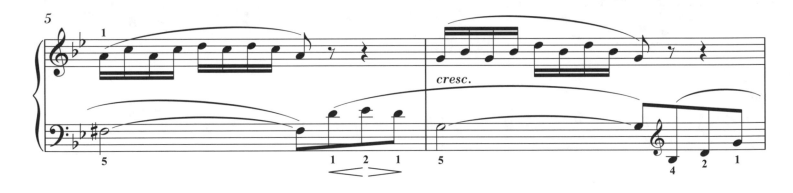

Edited and with fingering by Margaret Otwell.

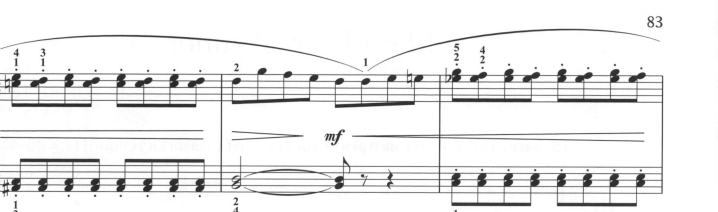

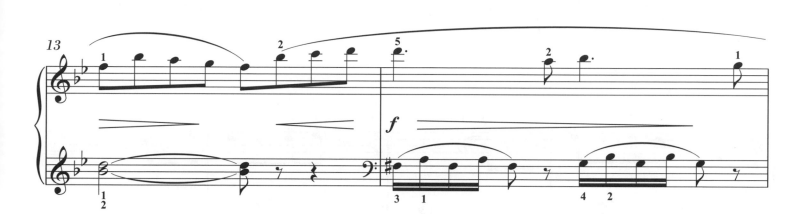

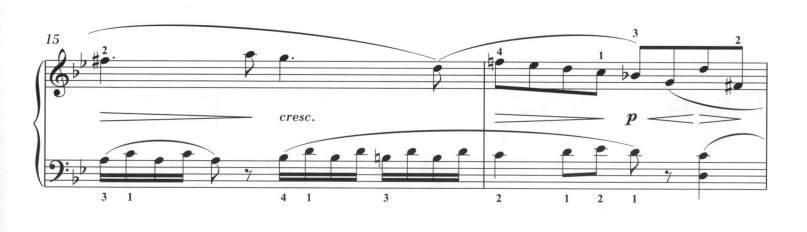

Mazurka in D minor
from *Album for the Young*

Pyotr Il'yich Tchaikovsky
Op. 39, No. 11

Не очень скоро (темп мазурки) [Not very fast (Mazurka tempo)] (♩. = 45–50)

Edited and with fingering by Alexandre Dossin.

The Little Wanderer
(Der kleine Wandersmann)
from *Albumleaves for the Young*
(*Albumblätter für die Jugend*)

Cornelius Gurlitt
Op. 101, No. 12

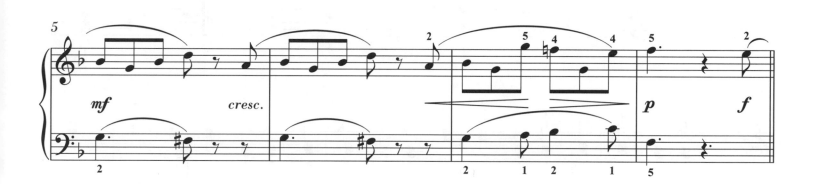

Edited and with fingering by Margaret Otwell.

Restlessness

(Inquiétude)

from *25 Progressive Studies*

(*25 Études faciles et progressive*)

Johann Friedrich Burgmüller
Op. 100, No. 18

Edited and with fingering by Margaret Otwell.

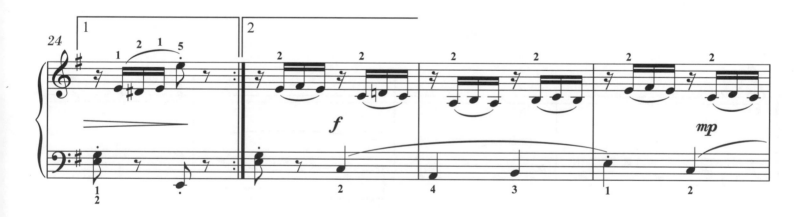

Hunting Song

(Jagdstück)

from *Albumleaves for the Young*
(*Albumblätter für die Jugend*)

Cornelius Gurlitt
Op. 101, No. 19

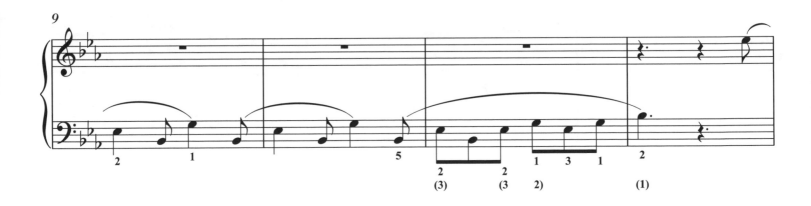

Edited and with fingering by Margaret Otwell.

Hunting Song

(Jägerliedchen)

from *Album for the Young*
(*Album für die Jugend*)

Robert Schumann
Op. 68, No. 7

Frisch und fröhlich
Briskly and merrily

Edited and with fingering by Jennifer Linn.

The Dead Little Bird

from *Album for Young People*

Max Reger
Op. 17, No. 4

Andante espressivo

Fingering by Matthew Edwards.

Folk Melody
(Im Volkston)
from *Five Piano Pieces*

Carl Nielsen
Op. 3, No. 1

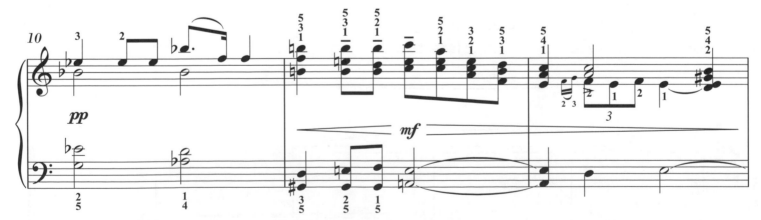

* Literally "humming" in Danish. It is unclear what the composer intends.
Fingering by Stefanie Jacob

Study in A minor

("The Avalanche")
from *25 Melodious Etudes*
(*25 Études mélodiques*)

Stephen Heller
Op. 45, No. 2

Edited and with fingering by William Westney.

Of Strange Lands and People
(Von fremden Ländern und Menschen)
from *Scenes from Childhood*
(*Kinderszenen*)

Robert Schumann
Op. 15, No. 1

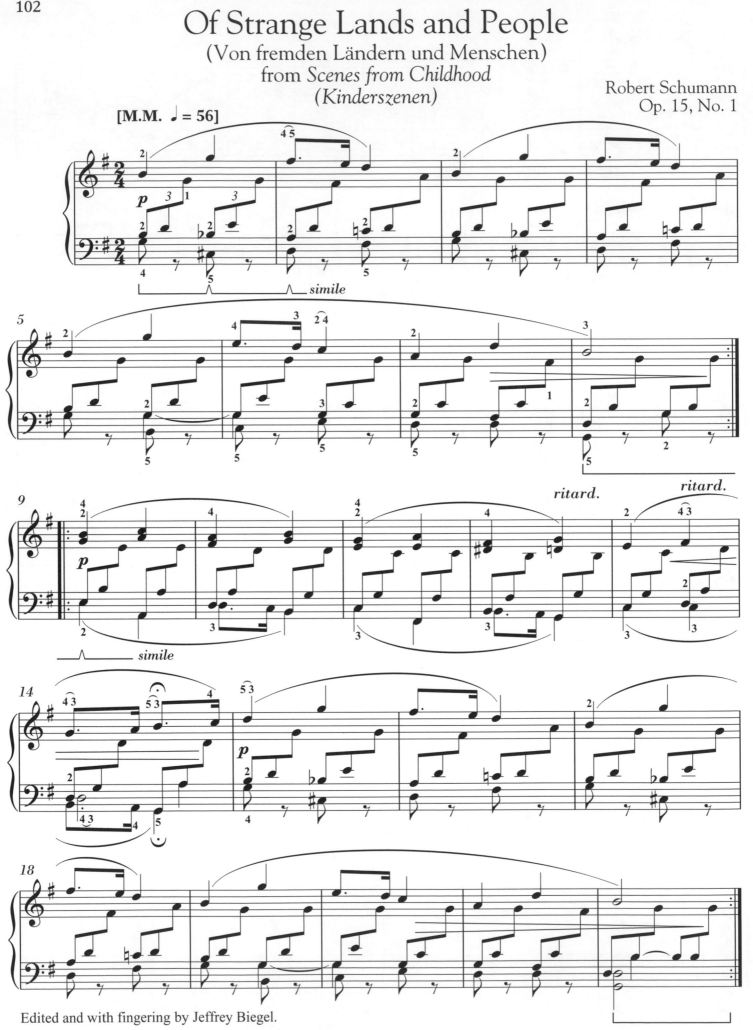

Edited and with fingering by Jeffrey Biegel.

Sweet Dream
from *Album for the Young*

Pyotr Il'yich Tchaikovsky
Op. 39, No. 21

Edited and with fingering by Alexandre Dossin.

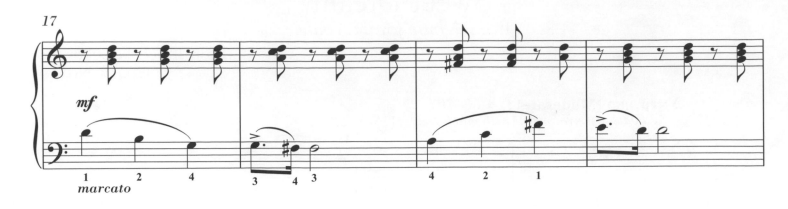

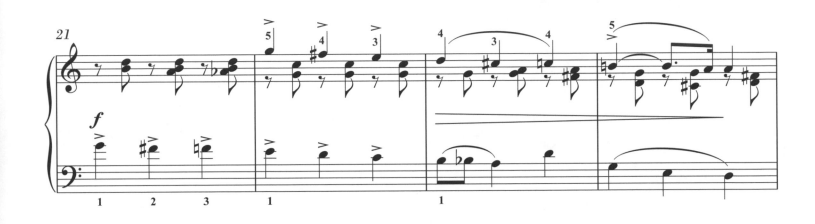

Waltz in A minor
from *Lyric Pieces*
(*Lyricshe Stücke*)

Edvard Grieg
Op. 12, No. 2

Allegro moderato [♩. = 56]

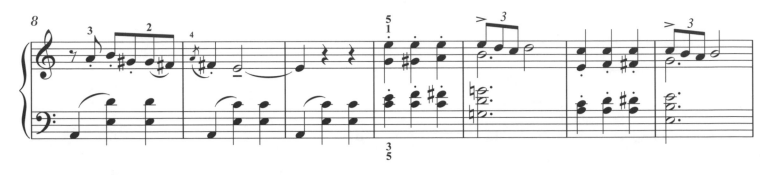

Edited and with fingering by William Westney.

*One might consider omitting the initial C-sharp from the left-hand chord in measures 39 and 47.

Confidence

from *18 Characteristic Studies*
(18 Études de genre)

Johann Friedrich Burgmüller
Op. 109, No. 1

Edited and with fingering by William Westney.

Little Romance

(Kleine Romanze)
from *Album for the Young*
(Album für die Jugend)

Robert Schumann
Op. 68, No. 19

Edited and with fingering by Jennifer Linn.

Prelude in A Major

Frédéric Chopin
Op. 28, No. 7

Edited and with fingering by Brian Ganz.

Dance of the Elves

from *Lyric Pieces*
(*Lyrische Stücke*)

Edvard Grieg
Op. 12, No. 4

Molto allegro e sempre staccato [♩. = 92–96]

Edited and with fingering by William Westney.

Prelude in B minor

Frédéric Chopin
Op. 28, No. 6

Edited and with fingering by Brian Ganz.

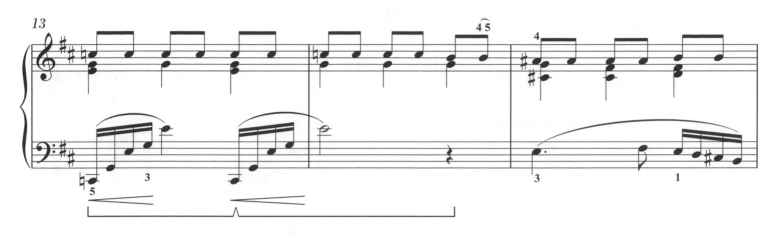

Puck

from *Lyric Pieces*
(*Lyrische Stücke*)

Edvard Grieg
Op. 71, No. 3

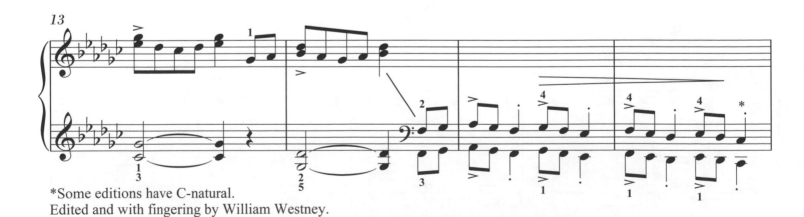

*Some editions have C-natural.
Edited and with fingering by William Westney.

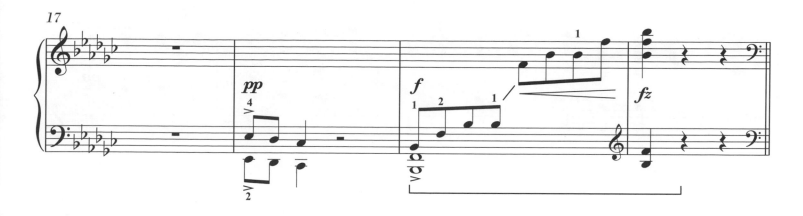

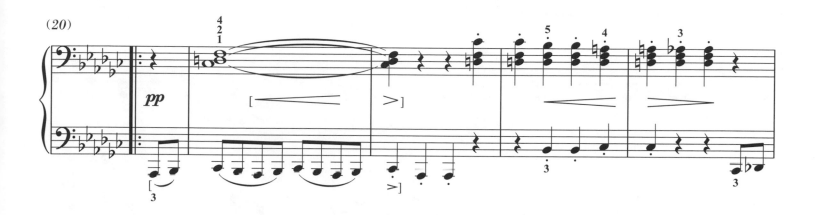

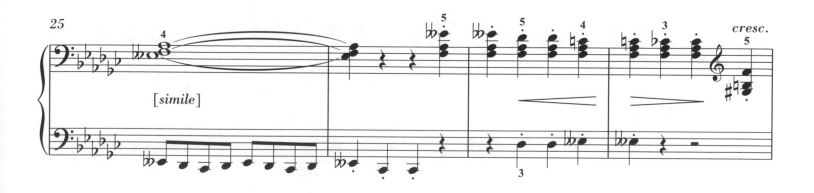

Prelude in E minor

Frédéric Chopin
Op. 28, No. 4

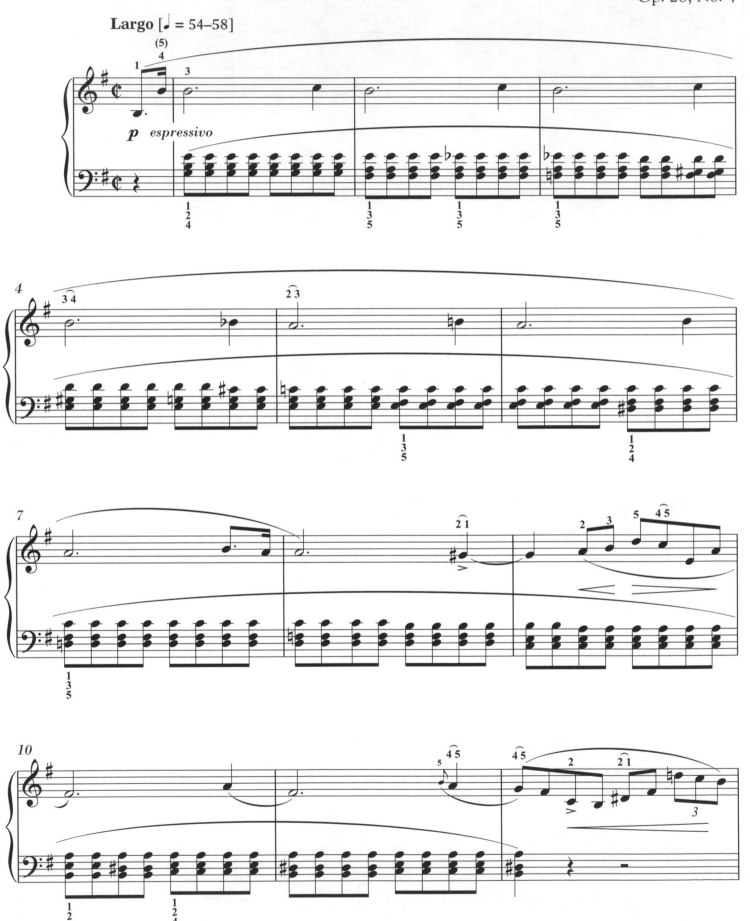

Edited and with fingering by Brian Ganz.

Arietta

from *Lyric Pieces*
(Lyrische Stücke)

Edvard Grieg
Op. 12, No. 1

Poco andante e sostenuto [♩ = 63–69]

Edited and with fingering by William Westney.

THE 20TH CENTURY

In Progressive Order of Difficulty

The pieces were previously published in the following
Schirmer Performance Editions volume:

The Chase
Clowning
Lyric Piece
Novelette
from *Kabalevsky: 30 Pieces for Children, Op. 27*
edited by Richard Walters

Slow Waltz
from *Kabalevsky: 24 Pieces for Children, Op. 24*
edited by Margaret Otwell

All other 20th century pieces in this collection are from
The 20th Century: Intermediate Level
edited by Richard Walters

Ivan Sings
from *Adventures of Ivan*

Aram Khachaturian

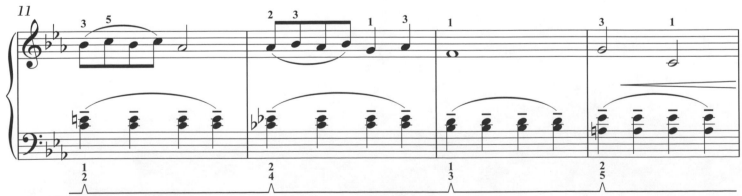

Fingerings are by the composer.

Slow Waltz
from 24 Pieces for Children

Dmitri Kabalevsky
Op. 39, No. 23

Adagio, tranquillo [♩ = c. 80–88]

Fingerings are editorial suggestions.

Round Dance
from *For Children*, Volume 1

Béla Bartók

Fingerings are by the composer.

Festive Dance
from *Five Little Dances*

Paul Creston
Op. 24, No. 5

Fingerings are editorial suggestions.

The Chase

from *30 Pieces for Children*

Dmitri Kabalevsky
Op. 27, No. 21

Fingerings are editorial suggestions.

Clowning
from *30 Pieces for Children*

Dmitri Kabalevsky
Op. 27, No. 10

Fingerings are editorial suggestions.

Rustic Dance

from *Five Little Dances*

Paul Creston
Op. 24, No. 1

Fingerings are editorial suggestions.

für mein nur Einziger Böski

Little Shimmy

George Antheil

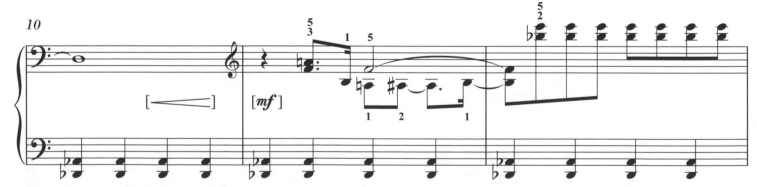

Fingerings are editorial suggestions.

Bagatelle No. 6

from *Fourteen Bagatelles*

Béla Bartók

Fingerings are editorial suggestions.

Birthday
from *Children's Notebook for Piano*

Dmitri Shostakovich
Op. 69, No. 7

Fingerings are editorial suggestions.

Lyric Piece
from *30 Pieces for Children*

Dmitri Kabalevsky
Op. 27, No. 16

Fingerings are editorial suggestions.

to Jean

Petite Berceuse

Samuel Barber

The fingerings in italics are Barber's.
Pedaling is editorial suggestion.

Novelette
from *30 Pieces for Children*

Dmitri Kabalevsky
Op. 27, No. 25

Fingerings are editorial suggestions.

Mountain Lullaby
from *Mountain Idylls*

Alan Hovhaness
Op. 119, No. 3

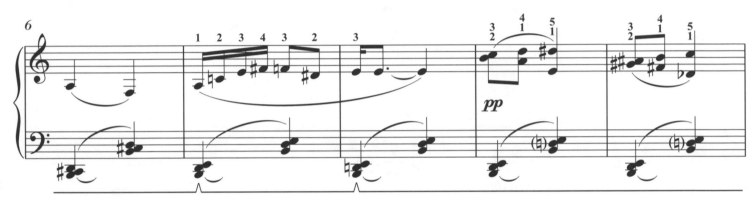

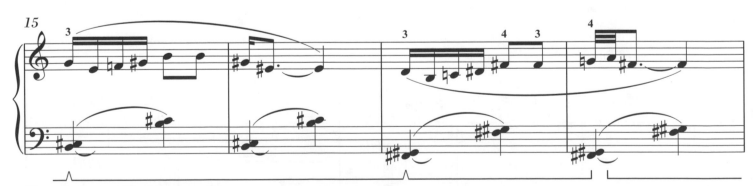

Fingerings are editorial suggestions.

Promenade
from *Music for Children*

Sergei Prokofiev
Op. 65, No. 2

Fingerings are editorial suggestions.

Regrets
from *Music for Children*

Sergei Prokofiev
Op. 65, No. 5

Fingerings are editorial suggestions.

Morning
from *Music for Children*

Sergei Prokofiev
Op. 65, No. 1

Andante tranquillo [♩ = c. 66–69]

[*with pedal*]

mf gravamente

Fingerings are editorial suggestions.

Jeering Song

from *For Children*, Volume 1

Béla Bartók

Fingerings are by the composer.

à Mademoiselle Jeanne Leleu

Prélude

Maurice Ravel

Assez lent et très expressif (d'un rythme libre) ♩ = 60 environ

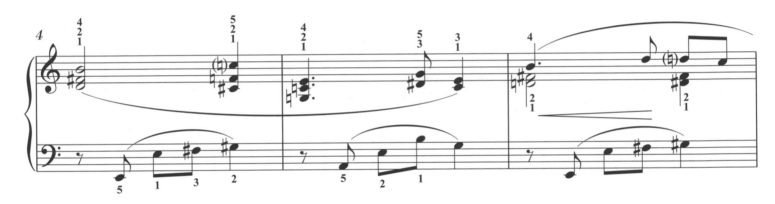

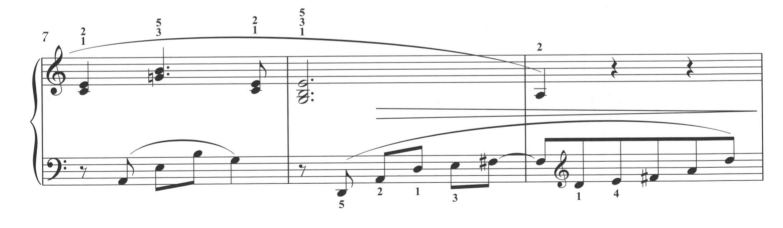

Fingerings are editorial suggestions.

to Number 220601

To My Steinway
from *Three Sketches for Pianoforte*

Samuel Barber

Fingerings are editorial suggestions.

Rondo-Toccata
from *Four Rondos*

Dmitri Kabalevsky
Op. 60, No. 4

Allegro scherzando [♩ = c. 154]

Fingerings are by the composer.

Fable No. 9
from *Fables*

Robert Muczynski
Op. 21, No. 9

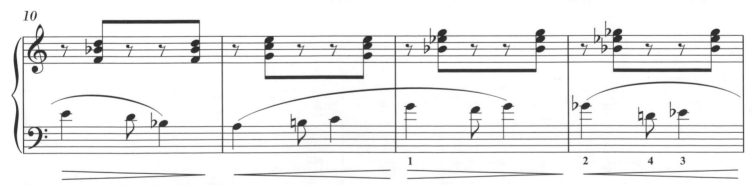

Fingerings are editorial suggestions.

Playing Marbles
(Bolinhas de vidro)
from *Children's Festival: Little Suite for Piano*

Octavio Pinto

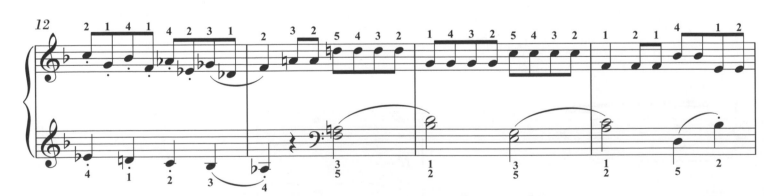

Fingerings are by the composer.